THE
REAL NAME
<u>OF</u> GOD

"*The Real Name of God* is theology that reads like a mystery novel. With scholarship, personal reflection, and wisdom, Rabbi Wayne Dosick points to what is in plain view but overlooked in sacred text: God's name is **Anochi,** "I Am," the source of life and the longing to love who transcends and includes all that exists. Guiding both a celebration of Jewish expression and universal belonging, *The Real Name of God* evokes a life-throbbing, spiritually uplifting call by **Anochi** to each of us."

RABBI ELIE SPITZ, AUTHOR OF DOES THE SOUL SURVIVE?

". . . provides us with a brilliant and crystal clear understanding of the all-encompassing God of love. Surely this is a much-needed message for all who are seeking a fresh and direct route into personal faith."

RABBI LEAH NOVICK, AUTHOR OF ON THE WINGS
OF SHEKHINAH: REDISCOVERING JUDAISM'S DIVINE FEMININE

"Rabbi Wayne Dosick once again reveals his passion for religion, his quest for the Divine, and his commitment for both plumbing the depths and scaling the heights of faith and belief. . . . He is fearless in his search for the spirit, as he explores meanings behind meanings and worlds beyond worlds. His combination of intellect and inspiration are alive, warm, and embracing."

DAVID M. POSNER, PH.D., CONGREGATION EMANU-EL
OF THE CITY OF NEW YORK

". . . introduces us to a holy interface with Divinity, a way for us to grasp humanly the utterly transcendent *Ein Sof*/Infinite God. How can we fulfill the *mitzvah* of our times, 'Love your neighbor as yourself,' without recognizing that the Holy 'I Am' is an essential partner in every loving relationship? Rabbi Dosick is a powerful teacher for our times."

RABBI SHAYA ISENBERG, PH.D., ASSOCIATE PROFESSOR
AND CHAIR OF THE DEPARTMENT OF RELIGION,
UNIVERSITY OF FLORIDA

THE
REAL NAME
of GOD

EMBRACING
THE FULL ESSENCE
OF THE DIVINE

RABBI WAYNE DOSICK, PH.D.

Inner Traditions
Rochester, Vermont • Toronto, Canada

Inner Traditions
One Park Street
Rochester, Vermont 05767
www.InnerTraditions.com

Text stock is SFI certified

Library of Congress Cataloging-in-Publication Data
Dosick, Wayne D., 1947–
    The real name of God : embracing the full essence of the divine / Wayne Dosick.
        p. cm.
    Includes bibliographical information (p.) and index.
    ISBN 978-1-59477-473-7 (pbk.) — ISBN 978-1-59477-691-5 (e-book)
    1. God (Judaism)—Name. I. Title.
    BM610.D67 2012
    296.3'112—dc23

                                                                                    2012001841

Printed and bound in the United States by Lake Book Manufacturing, Inc.
The text paper is SFI certified. The Sustainable Forestry Initiative® program promotes
sustainable forest management.

10 9 8 7 6 5 4 3 2 1

Text design by Priscilla H. Baker
Text layout by Virginia Scott Bowman
This book was typeset in Garamond Premier Pro with Copperplate used as the display
typeface

**Grateful acknowledgment is expressed to the following for their kind permission to
quote from their copyrighted text:**

Rabbi Shlomo Carlebach, of blessed memory, for his teaching "You Spoke to Us Once"
    from *Hu Elokeinu* from the audio tape U'vene Yerushalayim. Used with permission of
    the Estate of Rabbi Shlomo Carlebach. For further information, please e-mail Soul@
    NeshamaCarlebach.com.
Pax Christi USA for "O God, Open My Eyes" by Alan Paxton in *Peacemaking Day by Day*
    volume 2, copyright 1989.
The Rabbinical Assembly for "As God is Gracious and Compassionate" by Rabbi Jules
    Harlow. Reprinted with permission from *Mahzor for Rosh HaShanah and Yom Kippur*
    © Rabbinical Assembly, page 617.
Judy Chicago for "Merger." Poem © Judy Chicago, 1979. www.JudyChicago.com.
Rabbi Emanuel S. Goldsmith for his translation from the Yiddish of "If You Look at the
    Stars and Yawn" by Aaron Zeitlin.
Simon & Schuster, Inc., for selections from *A Corner of the Veil* by Laurence Cossé.
    Reprinted with the permission of Scribner, a division of Simon & Schuster, Inc. English
    language translation copyright © 1999 by Linda Asher. All rights reserved.

≈

For Ellen

Modern-day Prophet

Eshet Chazon—Woman of Vision

M'kasheret Olamot—Connector of Worlds

M'kasheret Z'manim—Connector of Time

Embodiment of Eternal Love

Channel of the Divine

Spirit-sister of *Shechinah*

Illuminator of **Anochi**

Voice of God

Heart of my Heart

Soul of my Soul

CONTENTS

PART TWO

DEVELOPING A PERSONAL RELATIONSHIP WITH ANOCHI

ACKNOWLEDGMENTS

I AM DEEPLY and profoundly grateful:

To God, whom you meet in these pages, for inspirational—and revolutionary—revelations, ever unfolding guidance, and sweet embrace.

To grand teachers and spiritual guides of the last two hundred and fifty years, who have opened my mind and heart to meet God in all the places where God is to be found.

Whether I know them from close up or from afar, whether from this World or from the Great Beyond, I am profoundly thankful to each and every one of them for their teachings and their influence:

- The Chasidic Masters, of blessed memory, the Baal Shem Tov, Rebbe Nachman of Bratzlav, Reb Levi Yitzchak of Berditchev, the Kotzker Rebbe, the Alter Rebbe, and the most recent Lubavitch Rebbe.
- The modern thinkers, of blessed memory, whose envisioning brought Jewish thought into the Age of Enlightenment: Franz Rosenzweig, Moses Mendelssohn, Rav Avraham Yitzchak HaCohen Kook, Martin Buber, Rabbi Dr. Abraham Joshua Heschel, and (he should live and be well) Elie Wiesel.
- The 1960 and 1970s Covenant Theologians, of blessed memory, who teach us of both the communal and the personal covenant:

my own teacher and Rebbe, Rabbi Dr. Jakob J. Petuchowski, Rabbi Arnold Jacob Wolf, Rabbi Dr. Steven Schwarzchild, Dr. Monford Harris, Dr. Emil Fackenheim, and (they, too, should live and be well) Rabbi Herman Schaalman, Rabbi Dr. Eugene Borowitz—whose incisive books best chronicle the evolving thinking of Covenant Theology—and the great contemporary Rebbe, Rabbi Dr. Zalman Schechter-Shalomi—whose fashioning of Jewish Renewal best embodies the spiritual beliefs and practices of Covenant Theology.

- Rabbi Shlomo Carlebach, of blessed memory, holy Rebbe and sweetest singer, whose passion for God and love for every seeking soul, gave voice to the Six Million who were so brutally ripped away from us, and reanimated and saved an entire generation through his inspirited song and deepest Torah teachings.

- Contemporary thinkers and writers, friends and colleagues, who have dared to take the first steps to bring God-talk back into the public arena. With some, I agree; with others, not very much. Either way, their work has challenged me, and, in some cases, brought me surety—in both directions: Professor Dr. Richard Elliot Friedman, Rabbi Dr. Arthur Green, Rabbi Harold Kushner, Rabbi Harold Schulweis, Rabbi Lawrence Kushner, Rabbi David Wolpe, Rabbi Mitchell Chefitz, and Rabbi Michael Gold.

I take great pleasure in expressing deepest appreciation and gratitude to these colleagues and friends—children of Spirit, each and all—whose knowledge, wisdom, critical thinking, and probing questions are reflected in this book. Each one agrees—or disagrees—with the ideas here to varying extents, yet, regardless of personal belief or practice, each has been gracious and generous enough to enrich the quest and the journey with kind and good guidance.

- Rabbi Micha'el Akiba for his wise, critical, and incisive guidance at the very earliest stages of the development of these ideas, and for his valued knowledge about Covenant Theology, from both Jewish and Christian perspectives.

- Professor Ronnie Serr in Los Angeles and Moshe Kempinski in Jerusalem, for their wise guidance in crafting the Hebrew for the new blessings and the Affirmation; my long-time cherished classmate and friend, Rabbi Dr. David Posner in New York City, for his deep knowledge and ever brilliant explanations of Hebrew grammatical forms; Professor Dr. Russell Fuller at the University of San Diego, for his deep understanding of the Bible, and for sharing his outstanding computer skills; Dr. William Finn for wisely suggesting placing Interludes between sections; and Dani Osborn for her close reading of the manuscript.

- The men and women of The Elijah Minyan and the *chavurah,* Shir HaYam in Greater San Diego, who listened and responded as these ideas were first developed and tested, and the good folks of the first Who Is God? and God Within classes, who wrestled with these ideas, probed and challenged with penetrating questions, and embraced the "hidden" God who has finally been found, and, then, re-centered their minds and the prayers of their hearts to the real Name—and the real Being—of the Whole, Complete God.

- My students at the University of San Diego who, coming mainly from Catholic backgrounds, asked, and asked, and asked about Jewish beliefs and practices. It was, in large measure, their combination of the blind acceptance that comes from a strict religious upbringing, the innocence and the rebellious arrogance of college-age inquiry and insistence, and their sincere desire for "truth" as it can be defined in a moment—only to change in the next moment—that sent me to deeper and deeper into academic and spiritual exploration of my own theology, observances, and faith. For their sake and mine, I was moved to seek out the answers to the contradictions and paradoxes that continually shouted to me from my main source text, and made the teaching of ancient certitudes demand contemporary discernment and discovery.

- All who read portions of the ever-evolving manuscript (some, more than a few times, as it went through its many iterations and versions), and/or had deep, far-ranging conversations with me, and offered thoughtful comment, criticism, and challenge. My precious son, Seth Dosick; the teacher of my youth, Dr. Irving H. Skolnick; my long-time friend and mentor, Rabbi Dr. Yehuda Shabatay, "my priest" and dear friend, The Rev. Fr. James J. O'Leary, S.J.; again, my cherished friend, Rabbi Dr. David Posner; my brilliant *chaver,* Rabbi Samuel Barth; sage-mentors Rabbi Jack Riemer and Rabbi Dr. Jack Shechter; and long-time friends and "kitchen cabinet," Joseph (Yossi) Adler, Dr. Steven Helfgot, Alan Rubin, and Aliya Cheskis-Cotel.

- Rabbinic colleagues, wise and wonderful friends, men and women of high intellect and great spirit—Rabbi Karyn Beth Berger, Rabbi Marc Berkson, Rabbi Diane Elliot, Rabbi Lynn Claire Feinberg, Rabbi Philip Graubart, Rabbi Sarah Leah Grafstein, Rabbi Dr. Victor Gross, Rabbi Vicki Hollander, Rabbi T'mimah Ickovitz, Rabbi Zoe Klein, Rabbi SaraLeya Schley, Rabbi Bonnie Sharfman, Rabbi Daniel Siegel, Rabbi Hanna Tiferet Siegel, Rebbetzin Neila Carlebach, Torah scholar, Sofer Alberto Attia, and our sage-elders, Rabbi Dr. Shaya Isenberg and Rabbi Leah Novick.

- And, in Jerusalem, wise and dear friends, all—Rabbi Joseph Schonwald, Rabbi Sholom Brodt, again, Moshe Kempinski, Rabbi Yitzchak Marmorstein, Ruchama Ben Avot, Student Rabbi Rick Kline, Emuna Witt HaLevy, Reuven HaLevy, Carmi Chai, and Alice Weisz.

- And sweet souls and wise advisors, Student Rabbi David Baron, Elisheva (Nicole) Rodgers Baron, Annie Klein, Amy Kazilsky, Benjo Masilungan, M.D., Carole Burke, Deni Phinney, William Phinney, Bea Wragee, June Carla Sinclair, Gary "Doc" Collins, Morty Wiggins, Melissa Ellen Penn, and Elaine Jesmer.

- The men and women of holy Spirit—from every place and spectrum in the communities of faith—whose words of endorsement grace this book, and whose collective support and enthusiasm for these ideas beckon us closer and closer to a world of Oneness.

- Cantor Kathy Robbins, who, in magnificent voice and great spirit, sings the chants on the recording and CD that are offered as a companion to this book, found on the website, www.GodisAnochi. com. These chants are intended to help enrich and enhance your spiritual journey in celebrating God and nurturing God Within. I have taken the melodies for most all of the chants from *"Mi'Sinai"* liturgical modes—Jewish music that is so entrenched in our souls and psyches that it seems as if God handed down sheet music at Mt. Sinai, and from liturgical and folk tunes from the last two centuries. The *Shiviti* chant was composed by Shoshana Cooper; *Ruach* was composed by Rabbi Shlomo Carlebach and made popular by Rabbi David Zeller, both of blessed memory; and "Eden Once Again" is from music composed by Rabbi Margot Stein, based on "Merger" by Judy Chicago. Many thanks to these dear friends for sharing their inspirited creativity and talent.

I am so very grateful to Linda Mackenzie, the inspired founder of HealthyLife.net; All Positive Talk Internet radio, whose station hosts my weekly program, SpiritTalk Live!, and, there, Jay Cruz, the extraordinary producer of programming. It was Linda's introducing me to Inner Traditions • Bear & Co. that started this book on its way to publication.

And at Inner Traditions, I have found new friends—consummate professionals, lovers of books, and champions of the World of Spirit. I am profoundly grateful to the visionary founder and president, Ehud Sperling, and his wonderful wife-partner, Vatsala, for their faith in me; to Cynthia Fowles, who first welcomed me and directs publicity; Jon Graham, the acquisitions editor, who embraced this book and advocated for its publication; the then assistant to the managing editor, Kristi Tate; the very helpful special projects editor, Erica B. Robinson; the brilliant and caring guide, project editor, Mindy Branstetter; the copy editor, Jennie Marx; and the enthusiastic publicist, Olatundji Akpo-Sani.

My gratitude is never-ending to my parents, Hyman and Roberta, of blessed memory, who, in abiding love, brought me to God and Torah;

and to my treasured son, Seth, who is both the receiver and giver of great love.

And, greatest of all gratitude to Ellen, whose amazing gifts of mind, heart, and spirit are enumerated in the Dedication to this book, who is so very precious to me, and cherished by our family and dear friends, by our congregants who adore their holy Rebbetzin, and by her thousands of clients, students, and grand-students, who treasure her. As Rabbi Akiba (BT Ketubot 63a) said of his wife, I say of Ellen, *"She'li v'she'lachem she'lah*—Everything I am, anything you may learn from me, is all thanks to her."

The ideas that I offer in this book are a result of a lifetime of seeking. The unfolding understanding that has ultimately led me here is chronicled in some of my earlier writings. I invite you to explore some of my books—*Living Judaism, Soul Judaism, When Life Hurts, Golden Rules,* and *20-Minute Kabbalah*—to see the evolution of my thinking, praying, singing, chanting, listening, wrestling, dreaming, envisioning, and opening of heart and soul.

Throughout my life and rabbinate—lived in the shadow of Auschwitz, in the rebirth of Israel, and in striving to forge the creative survival of American Jewry—I have been motivated and inspired by the very real imperative *"Dos leiben ez a choyv"*—"This life is an obligation"—to the souls from the past perched on my shoulder, to the men and women, and especially the children who are at the same time the inheritors and the transmitters of who and what we are, and to generations yet unborn, whose rightful and sweet inheritance is a faith and a community of both tradition and ever-evolving change.

It is an incredible blessing to be alive at this nanosecond in time, when all the spiritual energies and inquires of the past converge, when new openings bring us to a theophoric moment of new revelation. The thunder and the lightning and the trembling of Sinai come in new form. The awesome sound of the Voice, the murmuring of quiet whisper, and the delicate sounds of silence mean that The One still speaks, and we still "hear and do." I am heartened by the assurance of Saadia

Gaon, speaking of God, "In each generation, You make plain part of the mystery of Your Name," and by the *midrashic* teaching, "God said: 'My Name is according to My work.'"

On this soul-journey of spirit, I have felt the very real spiritual presence of *Eli'ahu HaNavi,* Elijah the Prophet, who, according to our tradition, will herald the "great and awesome day," of the coming of the messianic moment, when all will know that there is One God, One World, One People; when Earth will be Eden once again.

With the discovery of the real Name of God, with coming to know the Whole God, with embracing God Within, and with expansion into Oneness consciousness—with all that we now have and hold that we have never had before—my prayer is that Elijah's vision and promise will come speedily in our day. We've been waiting long enough. And God has been waiting too.

. . . and they shall all know Me.

JEREMIAH 31:34

Do not remain standing at the Outer Gate.
Enter Gate after Gate.
until you have reached
the Innermost Gate.

The Gates are made to be entered.

Do not remain standing at the Outer Gate.
The Gates are made to be entered.

RABBI JULES HARLOW

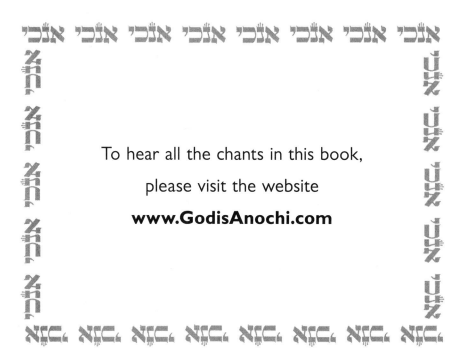

To hear all the chants in this book,

please visit the website

www.GodisAnochi.com

Note to the Reader on Writing the Word *God*

Except in the reading of the Scripture and in prayer, YHWH—the name that Judaism has always considered the "main name" of God—is not spoken, but most usually pronounced with a substitute name, and not fully written out, but signified with an abbreviation. Some even extend this practice to English, writing G-d (or G*d or G!d) instead of God. This is because the Name is considered so awesome, so sacred, that it should not be profaned or desecrated in casual or secular speech, or written on a piece of paper that might be easily or indifferently discarded.

I have chosen to write the real Name of God—**Anochi**—in full throughout this book and on its cover. This is because while the Name and the Being of **Anochi** is, indeed, majestic and holy, it is also the designation of the **God Within**, the God with whom each of us is in deep, personal, intimate, loving relationship. **Anochi**—the Whole, Complete, Total God is neither far off nor formidably untouchable, but close and dear. **Anochi** is our constant companion and our best and sweetest friend.

There is, then, no reason to put any distance between us, and every reason to always call and write **Anochi's** Name fully, completely, and joyfully.

BORN TO LOVE

———◄○►———

It happened, as it often does, on a star-lit night, when the
Heavens and the Earth were in perfect alignment.
They spoke the quiet talk of love, tinged, as love-talk often is,
with a bit of awe, and a bit of sadness.
Their words were, as words often are at moments like this,
of sweet sorrow.

"IT IS TIME."

"*No. No. Please don't send me away. Please don't make me go.*"

"Ah, My precious one, the time has come."

"*But I will miss You so much. And I will be so alone, so lonely.*"

"Never. You will never be alone. I love you, and I will never leave you. I will be with you wherever you go. I betroth you forever; I betroth you in love, and compassion, and faith."[1]

"*But I love You so much. I want to stay with You. And I want to stay here. It is so beautiful, so quiet, so safe.*"

"Yes. It is. But, the truth is that it is too easy for you here. I

have given you everything you need and want. It is time for you
to go out on your own; to make your own way."

"But, what will I do? How will I know what to do?"

"Before I place you in the womb, I choose you. Before you
are born, I consecrate you.[2] You are going on a special mission."

"Me? A special mission? You're sending me on a special mission? What is it? Please tell me what am I going to do."

"You know that I cannot tell you. It is something you must
find for yourself. But remember, you are not alone. We are partners; what I do is for you, and what you do is for Me. And always,
always know that I love you. And I promise you that I will watch
out for you, guide you, and protect you."

*"But I am afraid that You will forget me. You have so many
others who love You so much. Will You even remember me after
I am gone?"*

"Ah, My precious one. It is true and certain that when you
leave here, you will forget much of what happens here. Yet, now
and then, you will remember a smidgen or a shard, for, every
once in a while, I will give you a glimpse of what you once knew
and what, one day, you will know again.

"And I never forget. I remember you always. I will never forsake you. I love you, and I will always be with you. Do not be
afraid and do not fret. I Am never far from you. We can still be
with each other; we can still talk to each other whenever you
wish. Just call to Me, and I will answer you."

There was, no doubt, more to say.
But there was no more time.
Their embrace was sweet, but swift.
They began to move away from each other
in departure's delicate dance,
until even the fingertips of their
outstretched arms
could no longer touch.

Then, the Gates opened.
Heaven and Earth met and gently kissed.
And across the cosmos,
The Voice was heard:

"You are a child of the universe. You are My child—a child of God. I send you into the Void of Creation, so that you may come into Being. I send you to Earth to inhabit it and make it thrive."

PART ONE

THE MANY
NAMES OF GOD

ONE

HERE ON EARTH

HELLO.

I am Wayne Dosick.

Like you, I am a child of the universe.

Like you, I am a child of God.

And, like you, I know that the poet had it right: We come to this Earth, ". . . trailing clouds of glory . . . from God who is our Home."[1]

Our souls are eternal. They hold cosmic knowledge of all time and space.

But, the rules of being on Earth make it impossible for us to retain complete knowing. We forget; we cannot remember.

Yet, there is always a faint light in the shadows. Every soul on Earth retains sparks of eternal knowledge, and every now and then, we see a glimmer or a glimpse of what we once knew: an opening to All That Is.

Throughout the millennia, the way we human beings here on Earth have tried to stay connected to God is through what we call "religion." Every religion, every faith community, is a pathway to the Divine, a way of life that uses rational thought, sacred spirit, prayer, chant, meditation, movement, dance, and "the sounds of silence" to be with God, hear God's word, and do God's will.

For three major Western religions, the story of the first encounter with God, the "genesis" (pun intended) of our relationship with God, is in the "Go(o)d Book," the Bible—first in its original Hebrew, and then in scores of translations. The Bible is the source text for religious belief and practice, and is recognized as the premiere and foundational masterpiece of Western civilization.

The Bible is beloved by many because it touches minds and hearts; it tells the story of God, the universe, and humankind—the record of our history, the blueprint for our existence, and the design for our destiny.

Even in our contemporary highly rational, scientific, technological age, the faith-based Bible captures the imagination of spiritual seekers and rational empiricists, of people of every religion and of no religion, of every faith and of no faith, of everyone who recognizes the Bible's tremendous impact on human life and civilization. It remains of great interest and import to people and societies throughout the world, and to everyone who has ever wondered about God.

YET

Not long ago, a six- or seven-year-old boy said to me, "You're a rabbi, right?"

"Yes," I answered.

"So you believe all the stuff that the Bible says, right?"

Not wanting to go into all the intricacies of modern biblical scholarship with this young man, I simply replied, "Yes."

"Well then," he said, "you're a fool."

Taken aback by his boldness, yet intrigued by his certainty, I asked, "Why?"

"Well," he said, "you know that the Bible isn't true, it isn't right."

"What do you mean?"

"Well, not all the stories are true, and some of the stories are mixed up—part of a story here, part of a story there; some stories have their own beginnings, but endings from other stories. Sometimes the stories are true, but a lot of them are just lies—they're just made up."

Rather stunned, I asked, "How do you know all this?"

The young man stared at me with a look that seemed to say: You just don't get it; you don't understand.

And, then, he pointed his thumb upward.

"What does that mean?" I asked.

"I know about the Bible better than you do," he said, "because I just came from there."

"Where?"

"Up there. With God. I just came from there, and I know the real stories from the Bible—the way they really happened—because they were my bedtimes stories."

Perhaps that is why, despite all its acclaim and the affectionate loyalty it engenders, some consider the Bible—especially its first five books, the Torah—to be disturbing and disquieting; its tales and accounts pure fantasy, its characters seriously flawed, its main character demanding and capricious, and its lessons holding little if any moral authority or suasion. Throughout its long and storied history, many have seen the Bible not as a fount of guidance and inspiration, but as a source of conflict and strife between peoples and communities across the globe.

The "God stories"—and thus, many of the Bible's stories and teachings—are inconsistent and paradoxical.

In one glorious aspect, the God of the Bible creates human beings in the image of the Divine, celebrates the human spirit, gives grand and majestic laws for the highest ethical behavior, invites human beings to be partners in the work of the ongoing creation and betterment of the world, makes even the most mundane human interaction sacred, and elevates the ordinary to the holy.

Yet, those noble aspects of God are far too often overshadowed by a God who is—in great part—a rigid, militaristic, hierarchical, male authoritarian. It is a God who brings plagues, and kills firstborn; throws temper tantrums, and metes out harsh punishments; opens the ground to swallow up opponents, and makes war to obliterate enemy nations. It is a God who gets angry, is jealous and vengeful, makes outrageous demands, and—frankly—behaves very badly. It is a God in whose "name"—in later manifestations—is sanctioned evildoing and atrocity, warfare, crusades, inquisitions, holy wars, slaughter, and genocide; in whose "name" is preached fire and brimstone, hell and damnation. It is a God who, for many, holds the image of an old man with a long white beard, sitting on a Heavenly throne in exacting judgment, and writing, frighteningly, in the "Book of Life or Death."

Add to this the age-old question, now wrapped in contemporary garb: How can a compassionate, loving God permit little children to be born deformed and disabled; young mothers to have cancer and young fathers to drop dead; young women to be mugged, raped, and murdered; thousands to be swept away to their deaths by fire, earthquake, and flood? How can a just God sit idly by while millions wallow in poverty, are ravaged by disease, and starve to death? How can we believe in an all-knowing, all-powerful God who does not stop the brutal slaughter of millions, or protect little babies from being burned up in ovens of the Holocaust?

Add to all of this the challenges posed by this highly scientific, technological postmodern age, where so much power to manipulate and control the universe seems to be concentrated in human hands, so that, for many, the place and role of God is inconsequential or entirely moot.

God—the One I know personally and intimately, the God I remember from "before"—is total perfection and pure love. In my own life, and the lives of so many others, I have experienced and witnessed this God who creates and sustains me and the world; acts in grace; cares for me, protects, and comforts me; listens and responds when I call; lifts me up from the depths; catches my bitter tears and shares my greatest joys; gives me wisdom, guidance, strength, fortitude, hope, kindness, and compassion; teaches me eternal truth; inspires me to the good and the right; balances justice with sweet and tender mercy; redeems me and the world; cradles me in unconditional and everlasting love.

There is clearly a dissonance, a disjunction, a disconnection, between the God we remember before we came to Earth, and the One we often meet in the Bible, and whom we perceive acting—or failing to act—in this Earthly world of ours. Many have great difficulty reconciling the Bible's harsh God and the seemingly indifferent—or silent—God of good and evil, with the God of goodness, righteousness, mercy, and love.

With these swirling contradictions, we are moved to ask: Who are you, God? Are you the Bible's loving, nurturing God, or are you the Bible's harsh, fickle God? Will the real God please identify YourSelf?

Recognizing that the Bible is an evolutionary document, representing . . . an ongoing search for the Divine, the texts tell us more about our quest for God than about God's demands of us.[2]

Thus, we wonder: Do we find in Torah—as many believe—the true, perfect God, and God's exact and indisputable word? Or do we find the fears, expectations, and hopes of human beings projected onto an entity called "God"? Or is the Bible—in words attributed to the poet, Robert Bly—merely "a myth [that] is a truth frozen in a story"?[3]

WHO IS GOD?

Throughout the centuries, evolving theologies of Judaism, Christianity, and Islam have attempted—sometimes, very successfully—to meld God's seemingly contradictory nature.

The Jewish mystics focus on God who loves and embraces. In its beginnings, Christianity tried to balance the demanding, law-giving God with a God of love; a God who has three inseparable yet distinct faces—Father, Son, and Holy Spirit. Islam tried to synthesize the God of law and the God of love by proclaiming One (newly named) Godhead (with ninety-nine attributic names) but succeeded, rather, in providing a third vision of God. In the Far East, deeply spiritual Hinduism recognizes a large pantheon of Gods and Goddesses, with numerous names and characteristics.

There are those—throughout the ages and to this day—who, for themselves, have successfully integrated the many characteristics and behaviors of the biblical God into a satisfactory and satisfying relationship of belief and practice. Many dismiss doubts about God, because for them, God is the all-knowing, all-powerful, and absolutely perfect Deity, whom they love completely and unconditionally. Some even take their devotion to God to fundamentalist extremes, insisting that all others accept and embrace their unequivocal and unbending beliefs and faith.

And, still, there are also those who turn away from God, unable to reconcile the idea of an all-loving God with the image of the harsh, judgmental "old man"; thus permitting the God who "sends forth wrath" to eclipse the God of love and sweet holiness. And that is why for some, God is irrelevant and, for others, "God is dead."[4]

Over the years, I have served and taught so many Jews who either struggle with this quandary or politely ignore it. And, I taught Jewish Studies at a Catholic university, while one of my colleagues taught biblical studies at a public university. Both of us found that many of our students— Jewish, Christian, Muslim, and nonreligious—expressed great interest in the Bible and its teachings, and at the same time found difficulty in connecting with the God who is portrayed in that Bible.

This may be one of the reasons our synagogues, churches, and mosques are not overflowing with worshipers. When we go to pray, to whom are we speaking? When we seek God, whom do we find? When we read sacred Scripture, where do we find the God of "abiding love," rather than the God who is "a man of war"?

The increasingly popular rush toward "spirituality" holds the possibility of creating a personal relationship with the Divine, often by ignoring the biblical contradictions about God, and dispensing with the formal trappings of institutionalized religion. Yet, many find this approach too ethereal and amorphous, lacking the history, the heritage, the home-community and the soul-satisfying juiciness of a particular faith tradition.

There has to be a different, a better, answer—rationally, emotionally, and spiritually satisfying—that explains the wildly differing behaviors of God. There are plenty of old canards that just will not do: blind faith ("God has many different characteristics, and He can display any one of them whenever He chooses"); capriciousness ("God is God; He can do whatever He wants"); or resignation ("It's God's will").

There has to be an answer to the mystery of God's paradoxical character that we have not yet recognized or been able to comprehend.

And, here it is: While the Bible begins with the fundamental assumption that God exists, tells us about God's characteristics and attributes, about God's word and will, and about what God does, the Hebrew Bible does not tell us who God is. The Bible never answers our compelling question: Who is God?

Every name we have for God—including the Bible's "main name," YHWH—reflects one of God's aspects, attributes, or characteristics. None embodies the wholeness, the totality, the full essence of God.

None of the names of God that we know from the Bible—nor any of the names by which God is later identified and known—is God's real name.

And since, as the sage teaches, "You don't know something until you know its name,"[5] we have never wholly known the real God.

Picture a beach ball. A beach ball is made up of many different colored panels. Each panel is a part, or an aspect, of the beach ball. Without each and every panel, there is no ball. Without the existence of the ball, the individual panels have no role.

Now imagine that God is the beach ball. Each of the names we have for God is a panel of the ball—an aspect, or characteristic—of God. But, what is the name of the entire Divine Beach Ball, the wholeness, the totality, the full essence of God?

In English—especially in the so-called new age—the whole God is often called "Source." This makes sense, because we know that God is the "Source of All."

God is the everything of everything, the wholeness, the totality, the Oneness of the universe—male and female, light and dark and shadow, us and other, justice and compassion, pain and comfort, sense and non-sense, good and evil, anger and tranquility, indifference and passion, joy and sorrow, tragedy and triumph, right and wrong, yes and no, conflict and harmony, war and peace, vengeance and incredible love, life and death and life eternal. There is nothing that is not God. God is the Source of All. God is All. This is the absolute reality of God's Being— and ours.

Each of these aspects of God is like one of the panels of the beach ball: Sometimes we see displayed the panel that is goodness; sometimes, we see the panel of evil; sometimes harshness, sometimes sweetness. That is why it often seems to us that God is contradictory and inconsistent.

Unaware until now, our bewilderment about God is because each of the biblical names we know for God is only one of God's aspects—only one of God's many and varied characteristics—only one of the panels of the Divine Beach Ball. When we speak one of the names we know for God, we are actually invoking just that one characteristic of the Divine. Our confusion is that we have mistaken these individual aspects for the whole, complete God, for the full Source.

And so, despite having a multitude of names for individual aspects of God, we have never known the Bible's name for the full Source. Thus, we have never known the full, whole, complete God.

So, if we want to know the full essence of God, we need to know the Bible's real name of God.

Our challenge is to answer the simple yet profound question:

Who is the Divine Beach Ball?

What is the biblical name of Source?

Who is God?

EVER-STANDING AT SINAI

Is God's real name somewhere in the Bible, waiting to be discovered and revealed? Can we go into the Bible and find God's real name?

Interpreting and commenting on the Bible is an old and venerable practice. Throughout the ages, many illustrious and distinguished scholars of all faiths and traditions gave their explanations and interpretations of the text, so that today, we have a massive collection of commentary to accompany and enlighten the study of the Bible. Each commentator's interpretations are filtered through his (and in recent years, her) own historical, mythical, folkloric, religious, geographic, political, cultural, and social lens. Thus, even though each one reads the exact same biblical text, the understandings and interpretations differ widely and often profoundly.

Here in my own time and place, like a detective trying to solve a mystery, I have delved into biblical text: its language, legends, and laws, as well as its theologies, worldviews, politics, and social cultures. I have gone back in time to imagine myself in antiquity, in the beginnings of human consciousness on this Earth, standing witness as beliefs sprouted, creeds developed, and religions grew. I have sought to live in the heads and the hearts of the biblical authors. I have read the works of scholars, sages, and mystics of many disciplines and traditions. I have prayed, and dreamed and envisioned. I have listened and listened to the "still, small Voice."[6]

Here, with great excitement—and great humility—from the inner depths of the hidden, mysterious, mystical-spiritual level of Bible, and filtered through the prism of my own heart and soul, I offer my explanation and interpretation:

> The real Name of God that has been hidden from us for
> all these years is actually right in plain sight in the Bible.
> God's real Name is found!

By finding God's real name, we finally get to meet the whole, complete, total, real God: the supernatural, transcendent God of creation, revelation, communal covenant, and ultimate redemption; *and* the immanent God—the God Within—the God of deep, personal, intimate love.

While my teachings are sourced and steeped in solid, quality scholarship, and while I highly honor and respect the people and processes of both religious and secular academies of learning, it is not my intent to offer a classical academic inquiry—nor even to present or defend my ideas based on all the precedents of "traditional wisdom" that have come before.

Instead, this is a *sefer* (literally: "book," plural *seforim*), a book of sacred spirit, a modern-day exposition of holy teachings. It is my interpretation of our most sacred text, leading to my understanding of God. My findings come through the purposeful consciousness of hearing, envisioning, and imagining—abilities that God has graciously given me.

Therefore, this *sefer* stands in the lineage of the *seforim* of the God-centered, spirit-sourced teachers and rebbes* throughout the generations—of all religions, faiths, and traditions—who gave "new Torah" for a new time.

You may consider my ideas to be highly *chutzpadik*—bold, presumptuous, audacious. I hope that you will also find them to be revelatory, illuminating, and inspiring.

Ultimately, you will tell the tale. For, if you experience "Aha" moments of new understanding, if you resonate with these teachings, if the Bible is now more open for you, if you embrace God and your GodSelf with greater clarity and deeper love, then this will be your *sefer*, too.

So many wonder about God, and hunger for the sacred. So many would prefer not to be "turned off" by the idea of God or religious expression, and would welcome a pathway to belief and observance that makes sense and is warm and inviting.

Here, you will find God who is Oneness and Love.

You will find God, who brings continuing revelation, and awaits affirming embrace.

You will find that we, who are God's children, can eagerly enflame spiritual awakening and sacred renewal.

---

*A rabbi is an ordained clergyperson of any Jewish denomination (Orthodox, Conservative, Reform, Reconstructionist, Renewal). A rebbe is most usually a rabbi (although not always) who is a spiritual guide, a revered spiritual teacher, an illuminating soul, and sometimes an ecstatic. Most all the Chasidic rabbis are called "Rebbe." It is a term given by followers to acknowledge and honor the kind of rabbi this rabbi is, the place and effect that this rabbi has in their lives and the life of the community. If I say, "He is my rebbe," it means that he is my spiritual teacher and guide.

With newly honed insight we are able to explore pathways of mind and spirit that can bring each one of us into purposeful and meaningful relationship with God—the grand God of the vast universe, *and* the inner God of breath and soul and heart. So, the second part of this book offers you newfound spiritual skills and mastery, prayers, poems, chants, and meditations so that you can begin your profound inner journey toward God.

WHY NOW?

After being hidden away for all these centuries and millennia, why is this the moment to know God's real name, to meet the inner face of the Divine?

Even in an axial age such as ours—a time of massive and sweeping shift in the world order—a call to transfigure long-held, highly revered, and much beloved foundational beliefs can be threatening and scary, and can be readily scorned and rejected.

Yet, hearing, seeing, dreaming, and knowing God's word—what the ancients called prophecy—still lives. God's revelation is ever-continuing. In biblical imagery, the Bush always burns; Sinai is ever-present.

There are moments in history when accumulated wisdom and conventional thinking give way to the great leap of knowing beyond knowing: to the white spaces between the black letters, to the silence between the words. Human consciousness expands to discover and embrace what has always been there, but is only now discovered and revealed.

This is one of those moments.

"Behold, a time is coming"—that time is now!—"when there will be a famine in the land; not a hunger for bread, nor a thirst for water, but for hearing the word of the Lord" (after Amos 8:11). In our world, which often is in turmoil and feels confusing and chaotic, we hunger for the sacred, for meaning, for direction, for guidance; we hunger for the eternal. We hunger for God.

The Midrash—a compendium of Jewish legend and lore—teaches:

Every person has three names: one that a father and mother give, one
that his or her friends and companions call him/her, and one s/he
acquires (earns) for him/herself.   —TANCHUMA, *VAYAKEL,* 1

Every person's name—and, surely, God's—develops, grows, and
evolves over time and circumstance. Every name for God we have carries a particular energetic vibration that was the precisely correct God-
energy, the manifest Presence of God for our world at a particular
moment and place in the time-space continuum.

Now, evolving human consciousness—which has brought us to a
pinnacle of human intellectual, cultural, scientific, medical, and technological achievement—brings us to this pivotal juncture. As our world
moves closer and closer to the possibility of the "dimensional leap" that
will bring us to the time of transformation and evolution, redemption
and perfection, for our world—Eden on Earth once again—we need not
have merely individual attributes or characteristics of God. We need the
full spectrum of God-energy, the entirety of God's Being.

We live at this exact moment in the history of our world when the
eternal truth of God's real name that is embedded deep within our soul
memory, and the archetypal knowing of the real God that is at the depth
of our collective unconscious, "bubbles up," manifests, and is proclaimed.

Having God's real name, we can come to know the real God—the
Being, the Spirit, of God.

Now, when we finally and joyfully meet the full essence of God, we
can find our Home on Earth.

We come to a greater understanding of God's eternal plan and mission for us and our world.

We can find that every moment on Earth, as in the Heavens, we can
be in deep, personal, intimate relationship with God.

We can feel the sweet InDwelling Presence of God at the depths of
our beings, and be inspirited to celebrate God Within us.

And we can be beckoned to become even more fully involved co-creative partners with God in the spiritual evolution of the whole universe.

FOR US AND OUR WORLD

Knowing the real name of God will deeply affect biblical scholarship, reimagine world history, and reframe our collective and individual world views. It will impact us and our world in four significant ways.

1. The real name of God is genderless. Or, more accurately, it contains both genders—it is "gender-ful."

   Since God is neither male nor female, but the all-encompassing Whole, all of us who are created "in the Image of God"—especially feminists of both genders—will no longer have trouble relating to God who, until this time, has been almost exclusively identified as male.

   We will no longer have to wonder about—or struggle with—calling God "He," "She," or "It," and we will no longer have to be stuck in ancient ritual formulae that describe and address God only in the masculine.

   And, at this very moment in time, when the diverse forces of the universe are slowly but profoundly coming into the Oneness that will transform Earth into Eden, having the genderless name of God heralds the weaving together of the Divine Masculine and the Divine Feminine that is taking place in the Heavens and is being reflected on Earth.

2. The real name of God assures us that the God we meet in much of the Bible is not the real God, but rather aspects of the real God—aspects that may have been a necessary manifestation of God at a particular moment in time.

   For many, it is often difficult to relate to the aspect of God that seems to be angry, fearsome, vengeful and revengeful, hierarchical, authoritarian, militaristic, and often arbitrary. That wrathful

God—who kills firstborn sons, opens up the Earth to swallow those who have gone astray, and decimates enemies who deign to differ—is a Ruler with a "mighty hand," and seems to give or withhold blessings depending on how the Divine word and will is obeyed. For many, that God is still envisioned—from those old, childhood imaginings—as the old man with a long white beard, sitting on the heavenly throne meting out judgment and punishment.

Now we know: that is not the real God.

By knowing the real name of God, we can instead find and embrace God who creates and sustains us (and the world); cares for us and protects us; listens and responds when we call; lifts us up from the depths; shares our greatest joys; gives us guidance, strength, kindness, and compassion; teaches us eternal truth; inspires us to the good and the right; redeems us (and the world); and is our intimate friend who loves us.

3. The real name of God teaches us that God is not just the supernatural, transcendent God of the Heavens, the God of creation, revelation, communal covenant, and ultimate redemption. Knowing the real name of God enables us to know that God is also the immanent God Within—the God who is deep inside each and every one of us; who is in personal, intimate, loving relationship with us; and is our personal salvation.

   Because God is the very center of our beings, we can know God and be with God from "the Inside of the Insides." And we can embrace our own GodSelf, and bring more and more of that GodSelf—our God-like being and presence—to everything we are and do.

   And God needs and wants all of us to be part of the Divine; God wants us to reside at the Heart of All Being. Just as God is within us, you and I are within God. We are at the very center of God.

4. Most exciting at this moment in time: the real name of God is based in the Hebrew Bible, which is the shared theological source of all three major Western religions that trace their beginnings to Abraham—Judaism, Christianity, and Islam.

Thus, the real name of God is shared by all three religions, affirming a commonality and a unity that circumstance and situation have oftentimes caused us to ignore or forget.

Despite the many different and dear names by which we know God and that make God known to us, despite the singular and unique names by which individual faith communities call God, despite the very beautiful yet distinct paths to God that each religion creates, we know: God is One.

While Judaism continues to call God *Adonai,* and Christianity continues to call God Jesus, and Islam continues to call God *Allah,* we now have the One Name for the One God that we can all call God. Three faiths—One God.

In our contemporary world, diversity often threatens to tear us apart; togetherness and unity is the only path to righteousness and goodness, harmony and tranquility, and peace and love. Knowing and sharing the real name of God is a giant leap toward Wholeness, Holiness, and Oneness.

Despite living in a world that often seems to hang on the precipice of painful and chaotic self-destruction, we nevertheless live in a time pregnant with the possibility that the age-old promise of a messianic world of faith and love can be ours. We come with God to embrace and fashion God's greatest vision: The long-awaited moment when all God's children will touch hands in peace.

One God. One World. One People.

ON THE JOURNEY

Standing atop the mountain, Moses asked to meet God in deepest intimacy, but he was told that no human being can be with God *"Panim el Panim"*—"Face to Face"[7]—and continue to live on Earth.

So to Moses, the beloved servant, God offers an alternative. God tells him, *"V'samticha b'nikrat hatzur"*—"I will put you in the cleft of the rock, and My glory will pass by" (Exodus 33:22).

This will satisfy and fortify Moses, because, as our late beloved spiritual guide and rebbe, Rabbi Shlomo Carlebach *zt"l (zecher tzadik l'vrachah:* "The memory of the righteous is a blessing") reminds us, the Hebrew word *panim* has two meanings—"face" *and* "inside."

We know that one of the characteristic names of God—one of the panels of the Divine Beach Ball—is *Tzur,* Rock, meaning that God is strong and enduring.

So, what God is really saying to Moses is, "I will put you in the cleft of the *Tzur*—not just the rock formation that is on the mountaintop, but the Rock that is Me. I will put you in the midst of Me, inside Me. And that is how we will know each other: *Panim el Panim*—from the 'Inside of the Insides.' I know you, and now you will know Me at the deepest depths of our Beings."

This is how we, too, can know God.

That is why Reb Shlomo also teaches:

> *You spoke to us once on Mt. Sinai,*
> *but the whole world did not hear You.*
> *So, we are asking You, Almighty,*
> *speak to us once again;*
> *let us hear Your Voice just once more.*

> *But, this time, let the whole world see it,*
> *and the whole world hear it.*
> *And we promise You*
> *that the whole world will know*
> *that You are there;*
> *that You are God.*[8]

I joyfully invite you to the God Revolution; to journey, once again, to Sinai to discover the real name of God, and to meet God—"Face to Face."

TWO

THE NAMES OF GOD

אָנֹכִי אֹנֹכִי אֹנֹכִי

IN TORAH

THE TORAH—the Five Books of Moses, the first section of the Hebrew Bible—has eight proper names for God.

Elohim

In English, this name is most often translated as "God."

El

This name, meaning "God," is a shortened form of *Elohim*.

Shaddai

This name means "hills," or "mountains," and came to mean "breasts," implying the nurturing aspect of the Divine.

It is sometimes combined with *El* to become *El Shaddai*.

YHWH

This name is in the Hebrew consonant root-letters *Yud, Hey, Vav, Hey* that mean "to be," and that convey the idea of eternal existence—"was, is, will be."

Yah

This a shortened form of YHWH.

Elyon

This means "The High One," or "On High," or "Lofty One." This name is sometimes combined with *El* to be *El Elyon*.

Tz'va-ot

This means "Hosts," or "Whole Array." This name is sometimes combined with YHWH to be YHWH *Tz'va-ot,* or *Adonai Tz'va-ot*—Lord of Hosts, or Lord of the Whole Array.

Eh-yeh Asher Eh-yeh

When Moses asks God to identify GodSelf (Exodus 3:13–14) this is the name with which God replies. It is commonly translated as, "I Am That I Am," implying Eternity. "I Was. I Am. I Always Will Be." "I Am" is the God-Presence.

YHWH

Since the original Hebrew has no vowels, we can only speculate on the pronunciation. The rules of Hebrew grammar suggest the pronunciation, *Ya'ha'veh.* Objective scholarship most often pronounces and writes the name *Yahweh.*

A modern religious community chooses the pronunciation, *Jehovah.* Other possible pronunciations remain open to individual interpretations of vowel placement and sound on the four consonants.

Since this is the name designation for God that is most often used in the Bible, and since the pronunciation is uncertain, in this book we will not impose a sound designation, but rather simply write YHWH, leaving the pronunciation and sound to the ear, voice, and heart of each reader. YHWH is what the Greeks called the "Tetragrammaton," the Four-Letter Name of God.

Since the name of God was considered to be so holy, and not for casual use, a substitute name was given for YHWH when spoken: *Adonai,* which means "Master." So, whenever the word YHWH is written, it is spoken as *Adonai.*

In English, this name is most often translated as "Lord."

YHWH and *Elohim* are sometimes combined to be YHWH *Elohim,* or, in the spoken word, *Adonai Elohim.*

The name *Adonai* itself has taken on such sanctity that it too is no longer used in casual speech, but is now spoken only in reading of

Scripture or in prayer. Most often, *HaShem,* which literally means, "The Name," is substituted for *Adonai.*

Many of these names, in both language and form, are similar to— or exactly—the names of gods from the ancient Sumerian, Akkadian, Assyrian, Egyptian, Babylonian, and Canaanite societies and cultures.

The authors of the Hebrew Bible took in these names, Hebraized them, and gave them sanctified status in the Israelite religion, which would eventually come to be called Judaism.

YHWH—in its substitute pronunciation *Adonai*—is how God is most often named, called, and addressed in the reading of Hebrew Scripture and in the ritual formulae of Jewish prayer.

For an explanation of why the name YHWH—which was not revealed until the time of Moses (in the Book of Exodus)—is used throughout the entire Book of Genesis, please see the Notes for chapter 2.[1]

A most interesting question is why *Adonai* is the substitute name for YHWH, because, try as we might, there seems to be no way that any combinations of vowels with the consonants *yud, hey, vav, hey* (YHWH) can sound like the word *Adonai.* Most scholars assume that the sages who mandated the substitution simply chose an appropriate name to call God—"Master."

In a fascinating speculation, Rabbi Joel T. Klein, in his book, *Through the Name of God,*[2] argues that *Adonai* was the name of an Egyptian sun god, and that the Hebrew *Yud, Hey, Vav, Hey,* is the backward Egyptian hieroglyphic for that name. That is why, he posits, *Yud, Hey, Vav, Hey* is pronounced *Adonai,* and that is why, even today, many Christian churches have *Yud, Hey, Vav, Hey* written in sunrays high above their altars.

In another recent speculation, Rabbi Mark Sameth, in his article "Who Is He? He Is She: The Secret Four-Letter Name of God,"[3] argues that the name *Yud, Hey, Vav, Hey* should be read backward as *Hey, Vav, Hey, Yud.* This reading makes the sound, *"Hoo-Hee,"* which is translated, "He-She." Thus, Sameth contends that the Tetragrammaton—the Four-Letter Name of God—is not solely masculine, but holds both the masculine and the feminine. This reading affirms the notion of a God encompassing both genders. However, it does not account for the overwhelmingly male, hierarchical, militaristic, authoritarian behavior of YHWH in Torah.

IN PROPHETS AND WRITINGS

In the later sections of the Hebrew Bible—Prophets and Writings—God is called by many additional names. A few of the most significant are:

Av — Father

Shofet — Judge

Melech — King

Ro'eh — Shepherd

Tzur — Rock

These names characterize God's love, protection, power, and steadfastness. They are names given by the different writers of the various books in these sections of the Bible. Each name signifies the role at the top of the hierarchy of a particular category—Father in the family, Judge in the judicial system, King in the country or government, Shepherd in the agrarian world, and Rock in the physical world. The writers must have concluded that as these are designations of supreme authorities on Earth, they also must be good descriptors of the Supreme Authority—God.

IN JEWISH LAW, LEGEND, AND LITURGY

In Rabbinic literature—the *Mishnah,* the *Talmud,* and the *Midrash*—and in liturgy, there are scores more names for God. A few are:

Ribbono Shel Olam — Master of the Universe

HaKadosh Baruch Hu — The Holy One, Blessed Be He

HaRachaman — the Merciful One

Avinu Shebashamayim — Our Father, Who is in Heaven

Avinu Malkenu — Our Father, Our King

HaMakom — The Place, indicating that God is everywhere

Shalom — Peace, indicating that God is the ultimate Source of peace and harmonic unity

These names identify the characteristics, the attributes, the behaviors of God. In the words of the modern prayer, they "create an image in the minds and hearts, an image that souls can understand and touch."

All of the names of God, beginning in Torah, are masculine, both in their title or role, and in their Hebrew grammatical formulation. Since Judaism was born and developed in a rigidly patriarchal society that was dominated and controlled by men, the names of God generally reflect this masculine power structure. For example, the traditional name that reflects God as Parent is Father, not Mother; the name that reflects Ruler is King, not Queen.

Only one Torah name of God—*Shaddai*—hints at the feminine attributes of God, because it means "breasts," from the word for "mountain."

There is one name for God that was introduced in the Rabbinic Period (but not fully developed conceptually until much later) that finally acknowledges and celebrates God's feminine characteristics. *Shechinah,* the InDwelling Presence, reflects God's all-enveloping intimate nature that cradles in love, nurtures, and protects from harm.

The Kabbalists—the Jewish mystics—beginning in the thirteenth century CE, came closest to discerning the real name of God. They called God *Ein Sof,* which means "Without End"—"the Infinite One." They understood the wholeness, the completeness of the Divine; the entire Beach Ball. The evolving human consciousness of these spiritual mystics had brought them to the place where they, in their time, could name the essence of God.

For further discussion of the many names of God, please see the Notes for chapter 2.[4]

Still, the biblical name YHWH (*Adonai*) has remained the dominant name of God.

Following biblical tradition, once each year, on Yom Kippur—the Day of Atonement—the High Priest would enter into the Holy of Holies in the Holy Temple and speak the name of God—once in confession and prayer for himself, once for his family, and once for the people of the entire nation.

What name of God did he utter? Some say that it was the correct pronunciation of the biblical name, YHWH. Others say that it was a secret, mystical name. Either way, the name and its pronunciation were known only to the High Priest, and passed down from father to son as the priesthood passed through the generations.

> For a full explanation of the Yom Kippur ritual and its interpretations, please see the chapter 2 Notes.[5]

THROUGH TIME

Later, newfound Christianity will call God *Yeshu* (Hebrew); *Iesous* (Greek); *Iesus* (Latin); and Jesus (English from the Latin), meaning "Savior," and *Christos* (Greek); *Christus* (Latin); and Christ (English), meaning "Anointed One."

Still later, newfound Islam will call God *Allah,* perhaps sound-derived from *El* and *Elohim.* For Muslims, this is the personal name of the One, True God. At the same time, Islam has at least ninety-nine other names for God.

In another corner of the ancient world, Hindus continued to worship their many Gods and Goddesses, with their numerous names, based on the many characteristics of God.

Down through history, God has been given hundreds more names, both in myriad languages that people speak, and as a reflection of the ever-evolving understanding and presence and role of God in people's lives.

WHY?

Why are there so very many names for the One God?

Why does the One, All-Powerful, All-Present, All-Perfect God have more than one name?

The traditional answers:

- Different names indicate different tasks of God (such as: Creator,

Redeemer, Commander), and the different ways that people relate to God (such as: Parent, Ruler, Comforter).

- *Elohim* (usually translated as "God") is the generic name for a god, and YHWH (usually translated as "Lord") is the proper name of the God of the Hebrews. Thus, ". . . . YHWH (*Adonai*) *Elohenu,* the Lord, is *our* God . . ."
- The names "God" and "Lord," especially with little difference in the English meaning of the words, are often used interchangeably.

An answer through the ages:

- The many names for God reflect the multifaceted relationship that human beings have with God. To us, sometimes God seems distant and aloof, sometimes close and caring; sometimes angry and harsh, sometimes loving and comforting; sometimes capricious and arbitrary, sometimes measured and clear. The differing names we give to God are expressions of our perception of God's many characteristics and attributes. Just as throughout life, in ever-changing relationship, a child may call a parent Ma, Mama, Mommy, Mom, or Mother, our ever-changing relationship with God can lead to many different names that we call the same One.

The answer of modern biblical scholarship:[6]

- There are multiple authors of Torah, telling similar stories (Creation, the Flood, the Patriarchs) in different ways. In one set of stories, God is called *Elohim;* in the other, God is YHWH (*Adonai*). In the text, the two stories are sometimes separate, but are often intertwined.

Our answer:

- The mystery exists because none of the known biblical or postbiblical names for God is the real name of God.

THREE

GOD—FOUND!

THE MYSTERY is solved.

By reimagining and reframing the context of the Bible's original Hebrew text, and by retranslating the commonly accepted translations, we discover, and reveal the real name of God.

We will see that, in the biblical text, God's real name is expressed in two voices—the voice of God, and the voice of human beings.

When God's real name is spoken in God's voice, it is when God in the fullness of GodSelf—the wholeness, the totality, the everything of Source—comes to the fore, and reveals the great awesomeness of God's Being, and the very core of God's most important teachings and guidance.

And, when God's real name is spoken in human voice, we will see that it is when the speaker is fully in touch with the greatness, and the grandeur, and the soul-depth of the fullness of God Within.

We now can understand the identity and relationship with God at the depth of our soul.

SOURCE

Our first major premise in identifying the name of Source-God is that in Torah, *Elohim* is not—as we have always assumed—a name of God.

Rather, *Elohim* is the office that Source's representative holds on Earth.

The *Zohar,* the central text of Jewish mysticism, understands this when it reframes the opening sentence of Torah. The familiar translation is: "In the beginning God [called *Elohim* in this text] created Heaven and Earth" (Genesis 1:1).

The Zohar retranslates: "With this beginning, the Unknown Concealed One created the palace. This palace [office] is called *Elohim.* The secret is: 'With this beginning, He [the Unknown Concealed One] created *Elohim* [to supervise Heaven and Earth]'" (Z. *Bereshit* 1:15a).

So, "in the beginning," we experienced the full presence of Source in the Garden of Eden. But, after the fall of Adam and Eve—after the end of Earthly paradise—Source withdrew from Earth, and instead appointed an aspect of Source (a panel of the beach ball) to represent Source on Earth—to act as God on Earth.

Just as the modern electorate elects a person to hold the office of president, so Source appoints an aspect of Source, a "deputy," into the office of *Elohim* for a particular length of time and a particular purpose. So, in Torah we see the name and official title YHWH, *Adonai Elohim* much like we would see the name and official title, "President Kennedy."

The Torah itself provides affirmation. When God charges Moses with the task of going to Egypt to demand the release of the Hebrew slaves:

> *Elohim* spoke to Moses and said to him, "I Am YHWH (*Adonai*). I appeared to Abraham, Isaac, and Jacob as *El-Shaddai*, but I did not reveal to them My name YHWH (*Adonai*)."   —EXODUS 6:2–3

El Shaddai was Source's representative, holding the office of *Elohim,* for the purpose of establishing the covenant with the patriarchs. Now, a new representative named YHWH (*Adonai*) is entering into the office of *Elohim,* for the purpose of confronting Pharaoh and bringing the slaves to freedom. *El Shaddai* and YHWH are each an aspect of Source—separate panels of the Divine Beach Ball.

Throughout time, Source has appointed a number of different aspects of Source to serve in the office of *Elohim,* based on what human beings and the world require at any given moment. We have not met the whole God—Source—because, since the Fall, Source has never permanently put SourceSelf into the office of *Elohim.* Source has been hidden away from us—both in the Earthly relationship between Source and human beings, and, purposefully, in the text of Torah.

Now, with this new understanding, we can reimagine and reframe the Bible's original Hebrew text, and by retranslating the commonly accepted translations, we can now find the Presence of Source that was carefully hidden away in the Hebrew Bible; we can know the real name of Source.

THE HIDDEN NAME
REVEALED

Source—the real Name of God in Bible—is אָנֹכִי **ANOCHI** (pronounced **AH-NO-CHEE**; the "ch" is pronounced as a guttural, as in the name of the composer Johann Sebastian BaCH; the "i" is pronounced as a long "e" as in bee or see).

The accent is on the last syllable, **Ah-no-CHEE**. But, in more colloquial speech, it is often pronounced with the accent on the middle syllable, **Ah-NO-chee**.

Anochi is literally translated from the Hebrew as "I."

Picturing God as the beach ball, **Anochi** is **"I-Source"**—the wholeness, the everything, the complete essence of God.

Anochi is not an original Hebrew word. Its root is likely borrowed from ancient Sumerian, where the *Anunnaki* were believed to be the gods of Heaven and Earth.[1] In this pantheon, the head god, *An,* and his wife, *Antu,* had three sons—*En-lil, Enki,* and *Nanna. En-lil* had a daughter, *Enanna.* Later, the Akkadians elongated the name *An* to *Anu.* In ancient Egyptian, the three letters ANX (others say: ANI or IKI) mean "the living," or "alive"; indicating "Being-ness," which is surely the first requisite and characteristic of a god—the ability to convey life.

The Egyptian hieroglyphic character, ANKH, is the symbol of life—of conception, of a lifetime on Earth, and of the afterlife. A later Jewish text (*Pesikta Rabbati* 105–106a) teaches that the Hebrew slaves in Egypt knew this Egyptian word.

The *chi* (chee) at the end of the word **Anochi** is either taken for emphasis from the Hebrew word *kee,* meaning "indeed," or "surely," or it is possibly taken from a related Semitic language, where it is a suffix meaning "I."

There has been wide scholarly speculation and debate offered on the names of the gods of antiquity, but one characteristic is fairly clear: *An/En* is the basic name-sound of the gods of the ancient world. Coming from the so-called pagan world, this sound was recognized and embraced, and became the basis of the name of the One God.

The authors of the Hebrew Bible took in the name of Source from earlier civilizations, Hebraized it, and endowed it with the specific characteristics—particularly monotheism and covenantal relationship— that would make it unique to the early Hebrews.

In the Hebrew language, there is another word, *Ani* (ah-nee), that means "I." *Ani* is a simple declaration of first person singular—the small self, the personal ego.

Anochi holds the much more complex richness of "I, Myself; the Wholeness of My Being; the 'Me-ness of Me,' the full 'Essence of Source.'"

All this is affirmed in the word אָנֹכִי **Anochi** itself.

One of the beauties of **Anochi** is that it is a genderless Hebrew word. It holds the wholeness of both the masculine and the feminine aspects of God, the complete essence of Source, of **I-Source**.

Also, with the understanding that the formula of Hebrew grammar uses specific letters to indicate personal pronouns, the four Hebrew letters of **Anochi** represent:

א	aleph	I	prefix for 1st person singular
נ	nun	We	suffix for 1st personal plural
כ	kaf	You	suffix for 2nd person singular
י	yud	Me	suffix for 1st person singular

Herein is the totality of human relationships, making **Anochi** the ultimate paradigm of Martin Buber's teaching of the "I-Thou" relationship. For, if we can be in an "I-Thou" relationship with another human being, then surely we can be in an "I-Thou" relationship with the "Eternal Thou"—**Anochi**.

In the imagery of Hinduism, the "I-Thou" **Anochi** relationship carries the energy of "Namaste"—the God within me acknowledging the God within you; my GodSelf honoring your GodSelf.

The four letters of the Name **Anochi** also represent:

א	aleph	the awesome silence that precedes creation
		Aleph, the first letter of the Hebrew alphabet is silent; it carries no sound
נ	nun	the soul of every human being
		Neshamah means soul
כ	kaf	the majestic crown-place where God and humankind meet
		Keter means crown.
		It is also at the top of the Kabbalistic *sefirot*—the place where **Anochi** dwells, and where humankind travels to meet the Divine—where matter becomes spirit
י	yud	the merging, the union, of God and God's children into an eternal Oneness
		Yichud means union, connection, merging

And: using *gematria,* the numerology of Hebrew letters, the numerical value of **Anochi** (adding up the number assigned to each Hebrew letter) is 81, a perfect 9 times 9.

א	*aleph*	=	1
נ	*nun*	=	50
כ	*kaf*	=	20
י	*yud*	=	10
			81

In universal numerology, 9 represents universal wholeness and completeness—the very meaning of **Anochi** who is I-Source.

UNTIL NOW

Until now, **Anochi,** the real name of God has been hidden because

- If, as tradition teaches, God is the author of Torah, having dictated every word to the loyal servant Moses, then **Anochi** determined that the world—which was just meeting the One real God—was not yet ready for the whole God-energy.
- If, as modern scholarship posits, Torah was written and edited by multiple human authors, then those authors, well-familiar with the Mystery Schools of the ancient Near East, chose to keep the real name of God from the uninitiated, until all were ready to know the wholeness of **Anochi.**

Yet all along, scholars, sages, and mystics gave hints that they knew the real, hidden name of Source in the Bible.

The Midrash (*Pesikta Rabbati* 105–106a) says: "The first word of God on Sinai was **Anochi,** 'It is I.' It was not a Hebrew word, but an Egyptian word that Israel first heard from God. God treated them as did the king his homecoming son, who was returning from a long stay over the sea; he greeted him in the language the son had acquired in a foreign land. So God addressed Israel in Egyptian, because it was the language they spoke."

But, it is not just because **Anochi** is a recognizable Egyptian word that **Anochi, I-Source** invokes it at Sinai, but because it is the real name of God. The Midrash continues,

> At the same time, Israel recognized in this word "**Anochi,**" that it was God who addressed them. For when Jacob assembled his children around his deathbed, he warned them to be mindful of the glory of God, and confided to them that God would hereafter reveal to them with the word "**Anochi.**" He said, "With the word 'Anochi' He addressed my grandfather Abraham; with the word 'Anochi' He addressed my father Isaac; and with the word 'Anochi' He addressed me. Know, then, that when He will come to you, and will so address you, it will be He and not otherwise."

For further evidence that the sages knew that **Anochi** is the real name of God, please see the Notes.2

The common thread and the core of the sages' teachings is that God's revelation—and thus the perception and understanding of God—is fully given, but that it will not be wholly perceived until some future time, when human consciousness has evolved enough to grasp and meet the totality, the full essence, of God.

Now is that time.

Our own evolving human consciousness has brought us to the time and place where we are more and more able to sense those places where, in the Bible, **Anochi** inserted **AnochiSelf** into the human experience.

So, who is Source?
Who is God?
Anochi *is God.*
"I" is God.

FOUR

TORAH TELLS

THE WORD **Anochi** appears in Torah 141 times, in 135 verses.

There are another 218 appearances of the word **Anochi**, in 200 verses, in the second and third sections of the Hebrew Bible, Prophets and Writings.

By translating **Anochi** as **"I-Source,"** we come to a much greater and deeper understanding of the text, and a sense of the Presence of the whole, real God.

We see the crucial places where Source, **Anochi, I-Source** inserted the wholeness, the complete essence of God—the GodSelf of God—into history. These are the moments when no single aspect of God is enough; no deputy of Source can do the job. These are the moments when only **Anochi, I-Source** can act.

The most compelling example that **Anochi** is Source is in the opening sentence of the Ten Commandments.

Anochi YHWH *(Adonai) Elohecha . . .*

Which is commonly translated:

I am the YHWH (the Lord) your *Elohim* (God)
who brought you out of the land of Egypt. —Exodus 20:2

Using our new understanding, we translate:

> **Anochi, I-Source** appointed YHWH to hold the office of *Elohim* [God on Earth] in order to bring you out of Egypt. . . .

> **Anochi, I-Source** is the giver of the commandments; no deputy will suffice; no substitute can do the job. So that there will be no ambiguity and no question of their origin and their importance, the complete wholeness of God gives the ethical and moral blueprint for how human beings are to live.

The Ten Commandments continue:

> You shall have no other gods besides Me. You shall not make for yourself a sculptured image, or any likeness of what is in the Heavens above, or on the Earth below, or in the waters under the Earth. You shall not bow down to them or serve them. For **Anochi, I-Source** appointed YHWH (*Adonai*) to hold the office of *Elohim* [God on Earth].　　　　—Exodus 20:3–5

Anochi, I-Source is forcefully establishing the credentials of YHWH (*Adonai*). "YHWH is My appointed deputy," says **Anochi**. "Do not be fooled into looking anywhere else or into following or worshipping any false gods or their images. Be true and loyal to YHWH, for YHWH is fully authorized by Me and fully represents Me. And—continuing with the giving of the commandments—these are the laws that, in My Name, YHWH is giving you to follow and observe. Do them; do not be led astray."

Anochi could not be more clear or precise—or vehement—in giving YHWH the full imprimatur to act as God on Earth.

Another example of a well-known and compelling Torah text is the Jewish declaration of faith.

The text begins:

Sh'ma Yisrael YHWH (*Adonai*) *Elohenu,* YHWH (*Adonai*) *Echad.*

It is commonly translated:

> Listen, O Israel [Jews] the Lord (YHWH-*Adonai*) is our God (*Elohenu*), the Lord is One.

Using our new understanding, we translate:

> Listen, O Jews, YHWH is in the office of *Elohim;* YHWH is One (unique, alone, indivisible).

Now, the text continues:

> You shall love YHWH-*Adonai*, your God, with all your heart, all your soul, and all your might. Take these words *asher **Anochi** mitzav'cha hayom* to heart.

The last phrase, *asher **Anochi** mitzav'cha hayom,* is commonly translated:

> which I command you this day. . . .

Using our new understanding, we translate:

> which **Anochi, I-Source** command you this day . . .
> —DEUTERONOMY 6:4–6

Much, much later, when the sages formulated the Jewish prayer service, they made this biblical passage the centerpiece prayer—as both the declaration of belief in **Anochi**, and as the spiritual connector to the Divine. Then, for the second paragraph of this central prayer, they chose a passage five chapters later in the Bible, in order to affirm their understanding of **Anochi** as Source.

> It shall come to pass, if you diligently hearken to My commandments which **Anochi, I-Source**, give you this day. —DEUTERONOMY 11:13

When it is time to charge the people to love God and, later, to enjoin them to follow God's commands, it is not enough that the charge come from YHWH-*Adonai*. **Anochi, I-Source**—God, in the fullness of GodSelf—comes to give the mandate.

Two more prime examples follow—one from the beginnings of human consciousness on Earth and one from the beginning of the covenanted Jewish people.

The very first time in Torah when **Anochi** is spoken in the voice of the Divine is when God announces that a flood will destroy the world. **Anochi** brings creation, and because of the free-will corrupt and debased conduct of the people, **Anochi** could bring destruction. This is a moment of such great significance that it cannot be left to a representative to announce.

> For in seven days' time, **Anochi, I-Source** will make it rain upon the Earth. . . .   —GENESIS 7:4

In a crucial, history-changing moment, when God calls to Moses from out of the Burning Bush to assign him the task of going to Egypt to free the slaves:

> **Anochi, I-Source** Am the God of your fathers, the God of Abraham, the God of Isaac, the God of Jacob. . . .   —EXODUS 3:6

At this awesome occasion, at the Bush that burns but is not consumed, when God will identify GodSelf to Moses, and give him the world-changing task of confronting the Pharaoh and demanding the release of the Hebrew slaves, no deputy or aspect of Source will suffice. This must be the whole, complete Source, the fullness of **Anochi, I-Source.**

Indeed, the "holy happening" is so great that Moses is overcome. He "hid his face and was afraid to look at *Elohim*" (Exodus 3:6).

The use of the word *Elohim* here, commonly translated as "God," is affirmation that **Anochi** put **AnochiSelf** into the office of *Elohim* for this particular and most auspicious moment.

Yet, **Anochi** knew that only Moses was ready to know the full identity of **Anochi.** When Moses asks, "When I come to the Israelites and say to them, 'The God of your fathers has sent me to you,' and they ask me, 'What is His name?' what shall I say to them?" (Exodus 3:13).

Anochi does not instruct Moses to respond, "His name is **Anochi**." Unlike Moses, the people were not yet energetically or spiritually ready to know the real and full identity of **Anochi**. Indeed, it has taken all this time, to this very day, before we have all been spiritually ready to know **Anochi**!

Instead, **Anochi** says, "Tell them *Ehyeh-Asher-Ehyeh*, I Am That I Am; I Was, I Am, I Will Be; I Am Ever in the Process of Becoming" (Exodus 3:14).

For all these millennia, we have—correctly—summarized that the "I Am" Presence is God. Now we know: **Anochi** is the "I Am" Presence. **Anochi** is God.

Every time **Anochi** is used in Torah in the voice of God, it is when the fullness of God, the wholeness of Source, comes to articulate the most important core of God's teachings and guidance.

"I" IS "ME," TOO

Of the 141 usages of **Anochi** in Torah, less than half the time it is the voice of God speaking.

The others times the word **Anochi** is spoken in the voice of human beings.

This might tempt us to dismiss the assertion that **Anochi** is the real name of God. For, if **Anochi** is spoken by human beings, speaking in the first person singular, with the seemingly common meaning of "I," then how can it be the name of God?

Herein is the multilayered richness of the name **Anochi**.

Most of the time in Torah when a human being is speaking in the first person, the Hebrew word *Ani*—the simple form of "I"—is used.

In those instances when a human being uses the word **Anochi** to refer to self, it is used to denote the GodSelf of the human being who is speaking, the qualities and characteristics of God that are inherently embedded in each and every person.

From the voice of people, **Anochi-I** bespeaks the animation, the influence, the motivation, and the force that sets our true course and our true destiny as human beings.

Anochi in an individual human being—in you and in me—is **I-Source** within **I**; **God Within** me; my GodSelf within mySelf.

The very first use of the word **Anochi** in Torah is when the innocence of Eden has been shattered; Adam and Eve have eaten of the forbidden fruit.

Adam and Eve knew that they had violated God's instruction, and when they hear the sound of God walking in the Garden, they hide. YHWH *Elohim* calls out to Adam and says, "Where are you?" (Genesis 3:9).

God is not asking a question of physical whereabouts; God surely knows where Adam is. Rather, it is an existential question: "Where are you? What is happening? What have you done? What were you thinking?"

> He [Adam] replied, "I heard Your voice in the Garden, and **Anochi-I** was afraid because I was naked, so I hid."　　　—Genesis 3:10

Adam is still "warm" from being with God in the Heavens. He knows what it means to be the very first soul to come to Earth. Yet, he probably does not know the "rules" for living on Earth, for all he has ever experienced was the paradise of Heaven, and Eden on Earth seemed to be just like Heaven. So, he may not have paid much attention to God's admonition to not eat the fruit of a certain tree.

Yet, as soon as he does eat that fruit, his GodSelf, his **Anochi-I, God Within** becomes immediately conscious of his mistake, of his disharmony with his own God-ness.

Oneness has been breached; separation has occurred. Earth is on its way to being split from Paradise; exile from Eden is inevitable.

It is this disconnection from Source via our own GodSelves that we human beings have been seeking to heal ever since that auspicious moment. The discovery of **Anochi** as the real name of God, and the awareness of **Anochi-I, God Within**, is the first step toward that reconciliation, toward Earth being Eden once again.

In a most well-known verse, God asks Cain, "where is your brother Abel?" Cain replies:

Hashomer achi **Anochi**?

commonly translated:

Am I my brother's guardian (keeper)?   —GENESIS 4:9

meaning:

Am I responsible for my brother?

or:

Am I responsible for anything more than myself?

Cain is not being confrontational; he is puzzled. After all, he does not know the rules of human existence. He has never been taught about life and death; he has no way of knowing that his actions will lead to the extinction of his brother, or that he will be guilty of a crime. Cain, in his bewilderment, is simply and sincerely asking about the rules of life.

Am **Anochi-I** supposed to be like **Anochi, I-Source**? Am **Anochi-I** responsible for anything or anyone beyond myself? Am **Anochi-I** responsible for the well-being and welfare of other human beings? Am **Anochi-I** responsible for life and death?

These are the questions from the very beginning of human existence. And these are the questions that are still being asked today. These are the questions we ask when we are trying to touch **God Within** at the deepest place of our beings.

When the people of Sodom and Gomorrah anger God because of the debased behavior of the people, Abraham argues with God on behalf of the cities and their inhabitants.

> What if there are fifty innocent people . . . will You wipe out
> the place and not forgive it for the sake of the innocent fifty. . . ?
> —GENESIS 18:24

With great *chutzpah*—nerve, boldness, holy audacity—Abraham chastises God.

> Far be it from You to do such a thing. . . . Shame on You! Shall not
> the Judge of all the Earth deal justly?   —GENESIS 18:25

God demurs, saying that if fifty innocent people are found, the cities will be saved.

With that response, Abraham seems to suddenly realize how he has been speaking to the Lord of the universe. He seems to lose his bravado, and if not remorseful, he is self-chastising and humbled.

> Here, I continue to speak to God, *v'Anochi afar v'efer*—**Anochi-I**
> Am but dust and ashes.   —GENESIS 18:27

With this statement, Abraham seems to be acknowledging his humanness in contrast to God's Divinity, but by using the word **Anochi**, Abraham is affirming his GodSelf, the **God Within**, and drawing strength and fortitude from his internal God-ness.

His uncertainty vanishes. Immediately he, once again, begins bargaining with God to save the cities—what if forty-five, forty, thirty, twenty innocent people can be found? The negotiation ends at ten, but even ten innocents cannot be found, and God destroys the cities of Sodom and Gomorrah.

This exchange also is an early question of human existence that is still being asked today: Is my **Anochi-I**, my **God Within**, grounded enough in **Anochi, I-Source**, the transcendent God, that I am strong enough in my inner God-ness to be in dialogue—and even dispute— with **Anochi-I, Source**? Is my voice—as often and as consciously as possible—the voice of **Anochi-I**, my GodSelf?

The answer of Abraham of old is clearly yes. We can be inspired by him to understand and answer in the same way in our day.

When a human being speaks the word "**Anochi**," it is an expression of the highest level of human existence—the **Anochi-I**, the greatness and soul-depth of **God Within.**

It is an utterance—which is the object and the goal of our human sojourn on Earth—to be as God-like as possible.

Anochi-I is a word that we can all strive to be able to speak. Yet, there is a serious and profound caution that is stated clearly and unequivocally.

Anochi-I, God Within is *not* **Anochi, I-Source.**

I—and you—are *not* God.

We are *of* God, but we are *not* God.

In this "new age," some claim undifferentiated Oneness with God. That is *not* what is being claimed here.

The notion of **God Within** may lead some to believe that human beings are God. It is only in this time of evolving human consciousness that we can move beyond the ego-identification that "I" could be God, that **Anochi-I** might mean that I Am God.

Instead, we know that **Anochi, I-Source** is the supernatural, transcendent God. We know that God dwells within us as the immanent God, the God who is as close and as intimate as our very breath, but who maintains the singularity and uniqueness of the Divine Entity, the sole GodHead.

We seek knowledge of **Anochi**; we seek union with **Anochi.** But, we never forget: **Anochi** is God; we are **Anochi's** children.

Please never think otherwise; certainly, the teachings in this book are not "proof" of undifferentiated Oneness with God, and please do not represent them as such.

We celebrate our **Anochi-I, God Within**; we do not confuse or abuse its Presence.

For a full explanation of this concept, please see the chapter "Being One with **Anochi**," in the "**Anochi Within**" section of this book.

ANOCHI AND MOSES

Beginning in the Book of Exodus, **Anochi** appoints YHWH as **Anochi's** deputy on Earth, "I appeared [to the forebears] as *El Shaddai*, but I did not reveal to them My name YHWH [which I am now revealing to you]" (Exodus 6:2).

At the same time, the Torah introduces its other great protagonist and hero—Moses.

From here until the end of Torah, the Bible focuses on this primary relationship between YHWH and Moses because Moses is YHWH's mouthpiece and ambassador, and through this intimate relationship with YHWH, he models the fealty and loyalty to YHWH that is expected of the people.

With the daily interaction between Moses and YHWH, we see time and time again how **Anochi** inserts **AnochiSelf** into the most important moments in place and time. With Moses, **Anochi** has **Anochi's** longest-lasting and most intimate relationship with any human being on Earth, and through Moses speaks the most crucial messages of guidance, instruction, and inspiration.

Moses knew **Anochi** "Face to Face"—or, as we translate, "from the Inside of the Insides" (Deuteronomy 34:10). Through the "I Am" Presence and through YHWH, Moses encounters **Anochi** at the Burning Bush; he spends forty days and nights with **Anochi** at the top of the mountain, receiving **Anochi's** holy Divine Design; he stands in the cleft of the rock as **Anochi** articulates the Thirteen Attributes of God; he is in intimate conversation with **Anochi** as he leads the people through the desert on the trek to the Promised Land. "There has never again arisen a prophet in Israel like Moses" (Deuteronomy 34:10).

Anochi and Moses were most often on the same wavelength (we would say that Moses was such a perfect channel of **Anochi**) that it is sometimes difficult to determine who is speaking—**Anochi** or Moses.

There are a few precious instances in Torah when Moses says the word **Anochi** that indicates a merging of the human and the Divine for that moment in time.

When Moses is called from the Burning Bush to go to Egypt to demand the release of the Hebrew slaves, Torah reports:

> Moses said to God (*Elohim*), "Who am **Anochi (I)** that I should go down to Pharaoh?"   —EXODUS 3:11

What Moses is also saying, at the very same time, is:

> Who is [this] **Anochi**, who is going to confront Pharaoh?

Moses knew about the office of God on Earth—*Elohim*. He knew of *El Shaddai*, the God of his ancestors, who held the office of *Elohim*. He was about to meet YHWH, who was coming into the office of *Elohim*.

But, he did not yet know **Anochi**. He did not know the fullness of **I-Source**; he did not know the power of **Anochi, I-Source**. He did not know that **Anochi, I-Source** could appoint an aspect of Source to defeat the all-powerful Earthly king, Pharaoh, and Pharaoh's magicians and massive armies.

So, at the very same time, Moses asks, "Who am **Anochi-I** to go down to Pharaoh," *and* "Who is this **Anochi, I-Source** who is going down [with me] to Pharaoh?"

He will be assured that both he and **Anochi** are worthy of the task, and his mission will begin.

Here, the **Anochi-I** of Moses and the **Anochi** of **I-Source** have merged into one word—the full essence of God and the full essence of Moses.

Tradition teaches that Torah was given "by the mouth of God through the hand of Moses."

Throughout the Book of Deuteronomy, Moses reminds the people of their history, and of all the laws given by God. As he addresses the people, over and over again, Moses speaks in his own voice—his own **Anochi-I**. At the very same time, he is surely prophetically channeling the words of **Anochi, I-Source**. **Anochi-I** and **Anochi, I-Source** are merged in the one word, **Anochi**.

> And now, O Israel [Jewish people] give heed to the laws and rules that **Anochi** teach[es] you to observe, so that you may enter and occupy the land that YHWH, [who held the office of] *Elohim* for your ancestors, is giving to you.
>
> You shall not add anything to what **Anochi** command[s] you, or take anything away from it; but keep the laws conveyed by YHWH [holding the office of] *Elohim,* that **Anochi** commanded you.
>
> —DEUTERONOMY 4:1–2

Moses lays out a clear choice for the people:

> See, this day, **Anochi** set[s] before you blessing and curse: blessing if you obey the word of YHWH [who is in the office of *Elohim*] that **Anochi** enjoin[s] you this day; and curse if you do not obey the commandments of YHWH [who is in the office of *Elohim*] but turn away from the path that **Anochi** enjoin[s] you this day and follow other gods whom you do not know.
>
> —DEUTERONOMY 11:26

At the very end of his recitation, Moses says:

> Take to heart all the words which **Anochi** have [has] warned you this day. Enjoin them on your children, that they may faithfully observe all the terms of this Teaching.   —DEUTERONOMY 32:46

As when Moses prepared to go to Pharaoh, here the **Anochi-I** of Moses and the **Anochi** of **I-Source** have merged into one word—the full essence of Moses and the full essence of God.

By the end of his life, it may very well be that Moses has grown beyond relating to YHWH, and come into full relationship with **Anochi, I-Source.**

If so, then Moses is truly *Moshe Rabbenu,* Moses our Rabbi/ Teacher, who continually shows us the way to God.

YES . . . AND

As we read the most compelling of **Anochi** texts in the Bible, the evidence is becoming increasingly clear that **Anochi** is God's real name.

Now, we are ready to see **Anochi**—in even more manifestations— in the Torah, and in some of the most revealing and relevant passages in the rest of the Bible.

However, I realize that rather than being awed and delighted at finding that **Anochi** is the real name of God, some may be angry or disillusioned, or perhaps feel "tricked" into a belief in God that is based on less than "full disclosure."

Some may say: The ways God seems to behave in Torah may not always be pleasant or palatable, but God is God, and there must be a good reason for how God chooses to act. And, besides, this is *my* God, with whom I am familiar and comfortable, so I am willing to overlook any—humanly perceived—flaws.

Some may now be uncertain about God, for without having had the real name of God, they may ask: Who is the God of my history and traditions and holidays and observances? With whom am I in covenantal and personal relationship? To whom have I been praying?

Some may question the validity of the Bible itself. If the real name of God has been hidden away from us, we may now ask: What else is hidden? What else do we not know that, until now, we thought we knew?

Moreover, while the Bible is full of stories, the "Bible stories" we know and love—stories like Creation, and the Flood, and world chaos, and sister-wife and concubine-wife, and favorite son and sibling rivalry, and family deception, and blessing the firstborn—we may now ask:

Why are these stories (which we thought were sourced in a God we knew) any more special or true than the very similar myths from other ancient civilizations?

Is the Holy Bible really holy? Why should we continue to revere it if its stories are so common, and the real name of God has been hidden from us?

Within the questions are the answers. Tradition teaches: "There are seventy faces to Torah" (Bamidbar Rabbah 13:15). The pathway to God is multifaceted. Truth comes through myriad prisms.

First, knowing God's real name does not mean ignoring or rejecting all the precious names by which we have known and called God for millennia. Those names—particularly to faith communities—are holy. Throughout human history, they have been the way that people find and come to God, encounter God, talk to God, rejoice with God, weep with God, wrestle with God, and are guided, challenged, and comforted by God.

This is especially true of the name by which God is best known, the biblical name YHWH (*Adonai*). YHWH was the main and most lasting deputy of **Anochi**, placed in the office of *Elohim*. The Hebrew root for YHWH that comes from a verb of being—"was, is, and will be," signifies the eternalness of God, through all time and space. YHWH is the ultimate expression of **Anochi** in the now moment. God was and will be, and most significantly, God *is*—at this very moment, fully present and interacting with us and our world. The name YHWH will continue to be honored—and continue to be used by many when addressing God—for it has earned its esteemed place as a rightful manifestation of **Anochi**, until this time when the real name of the full Source, **Anochi**, could be discovered and revealed.

Neither does knowing the real name of God negate nor diminish the value and the merit of knowing all the names that are the aspects and attributes of God that make God and God's manifestations very real to us. Knowing the real name of God gives us the fullness and the richness, the vividness and the resonance, and most especially, the magnificence, of knowing **Anochi** in all **Anochi's** many faces and facets. The more we know of **Anochi**, the more we know of Oneness, love, and peace. Continuing to embrace and appreciate all the names by which **Anochi** has been known ennobles our lives. Knowing **Anochi** enlightens and enhances our lives.

Furthermore, it is the Bible that has survived to this day as beloved tales, as instructions for living, as a guide to right. It is in the Bible—even with all its internal textual difficulties, even when it bewilders us with all its conflicting accounts, even when we have trouble relating to its Divine hero—where we first meet God and open ourselves to faith.

It is the Bible that is holy writ—separate and unique from all other accounts. For in the Bible is the story of the real God—sometimes hidden away, sometimes represented by a deputy—and God's original blueprint and ever-unfolding plan for the universe.

It is the Bible that conveys God's word and will, including the greatest ethical mandate ever given to the world.

That is why the Bible has endured; that is why we learn from it, are guided by it, and cherish it to this day. Knowing that **Anochi** is the real name of God only makes the Bible deeper, more significant, and more precious to us.

FIVE

MEETING **ANOCHI**

אָנֹכִי אָנֹכִי אָנֹכִי

THE DIVINE VOICE

Throughout history, all of the **Anochi** texts in Torah in the Divine voice have been commonly translated with the simple "I."

Yet, now we know: in each instance, it is **Anochi, I-Source**—the fullness and full essence of the complete God—who is speaking.

Here are examples of some of the most compelling, most illuminating **Anochi, I-Source** texts.

Our interpretation and commentary will focus on why **Anochi** has chosen to insert **AnochiSelf** into the story at this particular place and time.

Abram (as he was called before his named was changed to Abraham) declared his belief in the One Lord God. This was the beginning of monotheism, and thus the beginning of what would eventually come to be known as Judaism, for the core principle of Judaism is the belief in the one and only One God.

Still, while he rejected polytheism—the belief in the worship of many deities—Abram knew that he, and for a long time those who came after him, would live in a henotheistic world—where he and his descendants would worship the One God, while acknowledging that others accepted and worshipped many other deities.

At this momentous time in world theological history, **Anochi**—

not leaving the task to any deputy, lest there be any confusion—assures Abram that his choice is correct.

> Fear not, Abram, **Anochi, I-Source** Am a shield to you; your reward
> will be great.   —GENESIS 15:1

For Abram, **Anochi** sets a vision of his descendants' future. They will be "strangers in a land that is not theirs, and they shall be enslaved and oppressed for four hundred years" (Genesis 15:13).

> but **Anochi, I-Source** will execute judgment on the nation they
> shall serve, and in the end they will go forth with great wealth.
>   —GENESIS 15:14

Once made, the covenant will be eternal. **Anochi**'s promise is that **Anochi**'s part of the bargain will be fulfilled.

Abraham finds **Anochi**. His son Isaac affirms **Anochi**. In the third generation Jacob is ready to go beyond the limited geographical area in which the family has been living. His compelling question: Is the One God whom Abraham has found, and with whom there will be an eternal covenant, simply a local "neighborhood god" like all the other gods of all the other tribes? Or is this God a universal God, who is with him always and everywhere?

The patriarchal stories of the book of Genesis contain a number of "travel texts," where **Anochi** offers assurances of universality.

> These major "travel texts" appear a little later in this chapter in the special sections, "The Double 'I': Mystery Solved," and "The Rest of the Story."

When Moses is reluctant to go to Pharaoh to demand the release of the Hebrew slaves a dialogue takes place between **Anochi** in the human voice of Moses, and **Anochi** in the Divine voice.

But Moses spoke to YHWH. "Please, O Master, **Anochi-I** have never been a man of words, either in times past, or now that You have spoken to Your servant. **Anochi-I** Am slow of speech and slow of tongue."

Moses does not believe that he, not even his **Anochi-I, God Within**, his GodSelf, is developed enough, strong enough, capable enough, to represent God before Pharaoh.

In the Divine voice, **Anochi, I-Source** counters, by telling Moses— in the same kind of "travel assurance" that **Anochi** had given to Jacob— that **Anochi, I-Source** will be with him and protect him.

And YHWH said to him, "Who gives man speech? Who makes him dumb or deaf, seeing or blind? Is it not **Anochi, I-Source**? "Now go and **Anochi, I-Source** will be with you, and will instruct you what to say."   —Exodus 4:10–12

Moses still objects, asking that someone else be **Anochi's** agent to go to Pharaoh.

Anochi counters again, telling Moses that his brother Aaron can go with him to be his spokesman.

You shall speak to him and put words into his mouth—and **Anochi, I-Source** will be with you and with him as you speak and tell both of you what to do—and he shall speak for you to the people.   —Exodus 4:15

There is no escaping an assignment from **Anochi**, for whatever the objection, **Anochi** will turn it aside. Seeing that he has no choice Moses agrees, and—reluctantly, but with a determined sense of purpose— makes preparation to go to Egypt.

When Pharaoh resists the demand and refuses to release the slaves, in anticipation of the plagues that will come upon Egypt, YHWH, through Moses, says to Pharaoh:

> By this you shall know that I Am YHWH [**Anochi's** representative]. Through Me, **Anochi, I-Source** will strike the water in the Nile with the rod that will be in My hand, and it will be turned into blood.   —EXODUS 7:17

Just before the freed slaves come to Mt. Sinai to receive the Ten Commandments,

> YHWH said to Moses, "**Anochi, I-Source**, will come to you in a thick cloud, in order that the people may hear when I speak with you, and trust you ever after."   —EXODUS 19:9

This is the prelude to the giving of the commandments, a task that as we have already learned, cannot be left to a representative or to any one aspect of Source. **Anochi** is the One to be known and trusted by the people.

We have already seen that at the majestic theophoric moment at Sinai, it is the voice of **Anochi** that introduces the Ten Commandments— "**Anochi, I-Source** have appointed YHWH to hold the office of *Elohim* in order to bring you out of Egypt . . ." (Exodus 20:2), and in the second commandment, "you shall not bow down to them [other gods] nor serve them" (Exodus 20:5).

The voice of **Anochi** continues:

> . . . for **Anochi, I-Source** Am an impassioned [others read "jealous" or "zealous"] God, visiting the guilt of the parents upon the children, upon the third and fourth generation of those who reject Me, but showing kindness to the thousandth generation of those who love Me and keep My commandments.   —EXODUS 20:5–6

This is quite a problematic text. Is God so demanding and jealous that punishment for disobeying the commandments stretches four generations into the future? What kind of God holds great-great-grandchildren responsible for the acts of their long-dead (and most probably never personally known) ancestors?

A traditional explanation is that misconduct—either denying God, or God's code of behavior—can have a long-lasting ripple effect that has a negative impact on the family name and reputation for generations into the future. At the same time, this traditional interpretation points out that the long-lasting effect of misconduct lasts for *only* four generations, while the reward for right-conduct lasts for a thousand generations.

The Kabbalists, the spiritual mystics, suggest that this verse means that in every third or fourth generation, a soul transmigrates—is reincarnated into a new Earthly body—to do *t'shuvah* (repentance, rebalance, and healing) for the previous lifetime in which the unfaithfulness took place.

With our new understanding that **Anochi, I-Source**, the fullness of Source, is speaking here, we read the verse through a new prism.

First, **Anochi** is teaching that YHWH—who had recently been placed into the office of *Elohim,* **Anochi's** representative on Earth—*is* a powerful, demanding, vigilant, and yes, can be a jealous and angry God.

The Israelites, who were receiving the commandments, had with their own eyes just witnessed the power and wrath of YHWH against Egypt—because Pharaoh had ignored, and then openly challenged, YHWH's authority and command. **Anochi** tells the Israelites not to be as naive or foolish as the Egyptians. Do not think that YHWH does not have the power to give you these commands, and to enforce them.

In a world where many gods were extant, YHWH's place and sovereignty were just being established. **Anochi**, the Source of All, says, "YHWH is My deputy; YHWH speaks in My Name. Reject all the other gods. Accept YHWH; accept YHWH's authority and embrace YHWH's commands—or there will be severe consequences."

And, therein, is the second explanation of this most notable verse.

Here—as will be delineated in other places in Torah—**Anochi** clearly lays out rules *and* the consequences for following them or rejecting them. **Anochi** acts neither randomly nor capriciously. There is a Divine plan that is clearly and fully explained. The Israelites—and all human beings who will eventually accept the commands of God—need not be confused or fearful. They do not have to obey or disobey commandments and wonder if there will be reward or punishment. **Anochi** says, "Here are the rules and, here, in advance, are the consequences." Choose to follow the commands—to do right—and this is the reward you will receive. Choose to disobey the commands—do wrong by being unfaithful to **Anochi's** articulated blueprint—and here, a priori, are the consequences you will face.

Thus, in the few words of this ennobling second commandment, **Anochi** affirms YHWH's appointment to the office of *Elohim,* and YHWH's power and authority; gives the clear intent and structure of how the commandments are to be followed; and lays out—for benefit or detriment—the consequences of accepting or rejecting the commands.

When the people are ready to leave Sinai after having received the Ten Commandments, **Anochi** says:

> **Anochi, I-Source** Am sending an angel before you to guard you on the way and to bring you to the place that I have made ready for you. Pay heed to him and obey him. Do not defy him, for he will not pardon your offenses, for My Name is in him. . . .   —EXODUS 23:20–21

The task of leading the people in safety and well-being through the desert cannot be left to a deputy. **Anochi, AnochiSelf's** personal messenger will be the guide. And, says **Anochi**, lest you think that my angel-messenger is only a deputy agent, I am warning you in advance: this angel acts as if it were **Anochi, I-Source**. Follow the angel for you are following Me.

In another telling of the giving of the Ten Commandments, which this time includes a recitation of the Thirteen Attributes of God ("YHWH, YHWH is compassionate and gracious . . ." [Exodus 34:6]), **Anochi** poignantly and powerfully reiterates the covenant made with this people.

> **Anochi, I-Source** hereby make a covenant. Before all your people I will work such wonders as have not been wrought on all the Earth

or in any other nation. . . . Mark well what **Anochi, I-Source** command you this day. . . . —EXODUS 34:10–11

As if witnessing the awesome theophany at Sinai were not enough, **Anochi** states clearly and firmly that this love-gift of the commandments seals an everlasting covenant between the Divine and humankind, here represented by the Israelites. Receiving the commandments gives the Israelites and their descendants the special responsibility of living, transmitting, and being the stewards and guardians of **Anochi's** will to all people through all time. This is the word of **Anochi**.

As noted earlier, very often when the word **Anochi** appears in the Book of Deuteronomy, it is "I" Within "I." Moses is speaking, but, at the very same time, the words of **Anochi, I-Source** are coming through him.

There are, however, two incredibly powerful times in Deuteronomy when **Anochi, I-Source** speaks alone.

When Moses is about to die, **Anochi** gives him the final instructions to give to the people before his death. **Anochi** is certain that the people will forget or ignore all the commands that have been given to them and become unfaithful.

> They will forsake Me and break My covenant that I made with them. Then My anger will flare up against them, and I will abandon them and hide My countenance from them. They will be easy prey and many evils and troubles will befall them. And, on that day, they will surely say, "It is because our God is not in our midst that these evils have befallen us."
>
> Yet, **Anochi, I-Source** will keep My countenance hidden on that day, because of all the evil that they have done in turning to other gods. —DEUTERONOMY 31:16–18

Anochi will disappear from the people, but it will not be because **Anochi** is forsaking them. It will be in direct response to the actions of the people. If they are unfaithful to **Anochi**, and turn away from

Anochi, then they will not be able to find **Anochi**, and **Anochi** will not be available to them.

This is not an announcement of a coming punishment. Rather, it is a declaration of cause and effect. The warning that **Anochi** tells Moses to give the people is simple: stay faithful to **Anochi**, and **Anochi** will stay with you. Be unfaithful to **Anochi**, and suffer the consequence that **Anochi** will not be found.

Sadly, **Anochi** was right. The people become unfaithful—they disconnect and separate from **Anochi** and **Anochi's** blueprint for human behavior. **Anochi's** countenance is hidden away. Only when the people reconnect and become "at-One,"* will **Anochi** reappear, and the covenant be made whole again.

Joshua, the son of Nun, is chosen to be the successor to Moses, to bring the people into the promised land.

> And He [YHWH] charged Joshua, son of Nun: "Be strong and resolute: for you shall bring the Israelites into the land that I promised them, and **Anochi, I-Source** will be with you." —DEUTERONOMY 31:23

Even with the gigantic task he is given, Joshua need not worry or fear. **Anochi, I-Source** will be with him as **Anochi** was with Moses. The mantle of leadership passes from one human being to another. The Eternal Leader—**Anochi**—remains forever.

THE HUMAN VOICE

Throughout all history, all of the **Anochi** texts in Torah in the human voice have been translated as "I." Yet, now we know: in each instance, it is **Anochi-I, God Within**—the deepest GodSelf—who is speaking.

---

*To "atone" for one's transgressions is a tenet of the relationship with **Anochi**. Here we use a variation on that term to show that atoning means striving to be "at-One"—fully connected, fully engaged—with **Anochi**.

Here are examples of when **Anochi-I** is spoken by a human being that are compelling, poignant, and most illuminating.

Our interpretation and commentary will center on why a person is speaking from the **God Within** at that particular time and place.

We see that each time **Anochi-I** comes from the voice of a human being, it is when that person is calling on the most important part of himself or herself: the GodSelf, the **God Within**. It is when each person is touching the greatest sense of connection to **Anochi, I-Source**, and seeking or expressing the very highest sense of humanity—wanting (or needing) to be God-like.

We see recurring themes of love, family, and especially human responsibility.

The issue of the barren wife is repeated a number of times in the stories of the patriarchs and matriarchs. Each time the childless wife speaks of her barrenness, it is from the depth of her being and sense of Earthly purpose, from her **Anochi-I, God Within**.

Sarai, Abram's wife (their names before the making of the covenant with God, when their names changed to Sarah and Abraham), is barren. In those times, the custom permitted the wife to give a handmaid or a consort to her husband for the purpose of having a child. The handmaid would be the surrogate; the child (for descendancy and inheritance purposes) would be considered to be the child of the wife.

That is exactly what Sarai does; she gives her handmaid, Hagar, to Abram to conceive and bear a child. But once Hagar conceives, "her mistress [Sarai] was lowered in her esteem" (Genesis 16:4).

> And Sarai said to Abram, "The wrong done me is your fault! **Anochi-I** put my maid in your bosom; now that she sees that she is pregnant, I am lowered in her esteem. . . ."   —GENESIS 16:5

Rashi (Rabbi Shlomo ben Yitzchak, France, 1040–1105) the premiere biblical commentator, explains that Sarai, in great part, blames Abram for her barrenness. "You prayed only for yourself; you should have prayed for both of us, and I, too would have been taken account of [by God] with you. And, furthermore . . . you hear my disgrace, but you are silent."

In this great emotional pain—brought about by her own barrenness, her handmaid's attitude toward her, and her perception of her husband's betrayal—Sarai calls out from the depths of her being. Her primal cry comes not simply from the place of her persona or personality, but from her sense of her mission on Earth, her reason for being—her GodSelf, her **Anochi-I, God Within.**

It is the same with the second of the matriarchs, Rebecca. She too is barren and "Isaac pleaded with YHWH on her behalf" (Genesis 25:21).

Note that Isaac may have learned a lesson from his father's failure to plea for his wife. Here, the husband's prayer to God is for the wife, and the prayer is answered: Rebecca conceives.

> But the children struggled in her womb, and she said, "If so, why do **Anochi-I** exist?" And she went to ask YHWH.   —GENESIS 25:22

After being barren for so long, Rebecca finally conceives—but the pregnancy is troubled; the twins fight in her womb. She is most likely in physical distress, and worried that the pregnancy might fail, or that the children might be born in compromised health.

So, her cry to God is from the depths of her GodSelf, her **Anochi-I, God Within.** What is my Godly purpose on Earth? Why is my GodSelf here, except to fulfill the mission of bearing children and carrying on the family line?

The Zohar adds that the *Shechinah,* the Divine Feminine, dwelt with the matriarch Sarah as long as she lived; when Sarah died, *Shechinah* came to dwell with Rebecca. This mystical tradition equates *Shechinah* with **Anochi,** because **Anochi** is the name for the whole, complete God, of which the Divine Feminine is an integral part. In her physical and psychic pain, Rebecca perhaps feels too small to seek out Source, so she turns to an aspect of Source, YHWH. The Zohar relates that she leaves *Shechinah* behind and goes to inquire of YHWH (Z. *Yayetze* 1:115b).

Does this "abandonment" of *Shechinah* contribute to the separation between Divine Masculine and the Divine Feminine? Does this move away from *Shechinah* toward YHWH contribute to the hiddenness of **Anochi**? We will never know for sure, but when we wonder, we can look to this moment in Torah history as one possible reason for the concealment of Source.

The theme of the barren wife is played out once more with the third of the matriarchs, Rachel.

Jacob comes to live with his uncle Laban in Haran. He is immediately smitten by Laban's daughter Rachel, and agrees to work for seven years to have her as his bride.

When the time comes for the marriage, Laban puts the "wrong bride under the veil," substituting Rachel's older sister, Leah, so that (as was the custom of the time) the older daughter will marry before the younger.

When the ruse is discovered, Laban agrees that Jacob can also marry Rachel, but he will have to work another seven years in "payment" for her.

"YHWH saw that Leah was unloved, and He opened her womb, but Rachel was barren" (Genesis 29:31). At this point in the story, Leah goes on to have four sons.

> When Rachel saw that she had borne Jacob no children, she became
> envious of her sister; and Rachel said to Jacob, "Give me children or
> **Anochi-I** will die."   —GENESIS 30:1

Rachel is clear: if she does not bear children, she may literally die from grief, but at the very least, her GodSelf, her **Anochi-I, God Within** will suffer spiritual death. Her life's purpose will not be fulfilled; her GodSelf reason for living will be extinguished.

This time, the third of the patriarchs dismisses himself from any responsibility.

> Jacob was incensed at Rachel, and said, "Can **Anochi-I** take the place
> of God who has denied you fruit of the womb?"   —GENESIS 30:2

Jacob's implication is that it is not he who is incapable of having children for he already has four children with Leah. It must be Rachel who is the barren one.

But far more, he is saying that even his own **Anochi-I, God Within** is limited. As much of God as we have within us, as God-like as we strive to be, we are *of* God, but we are not God. Jacob's GodSelf is not **Anochi, I-Source** the supernatural, transcendent, God. It is only **Anochi** who can ultimately create new human beings. On Earth, we are only **Anochi's** co-creators; the ultimate act of creation is **Anochi's** alone.

As compelling as that argument might be, Rachel is not impressed. According to the Midrash (a major compendium of Jewish legend and lore) when Rachel says to Jacob, "Give me children . . ." she adds, "Did your father act this way to your mother?" (Isaac who prayed for Rebecca) (Midrash Rabbah *Yateze* 6).

The sages teach that "God took Jacob to task for his insensitivity to Rachel. God said to him: 'Is this the way to answer an aggrieved person? By your life, your children [by your other wives] are destined to stand humbly before her son, Joseph.'"

Ah, the webs that we humans weave! The lives of our first three patriarchs and four matriarchs were filled with tension and drama and some not-so-nice behavior, and the themes of their lives played out generation after generation. Throughout Genesis, we see more of the same.

Yet, throughout their trials with their husbands, children, and God, the matriarchs are very clear and consistent. Their **Anochi-I**, their **God Within** craves the ability to bear children, and thus to fulfill their Earthly purpose. Their entire spiritual being—and, perhaps their very lives—depend on their **Anochi-I, God Within** reaching its highest God-like potential. As **Anochi, I-Source** creates in the Heavens, their **Anochi-I, God Within** must create on Earth.

When Abraham's beloved wife Sarah dies, he must find a burial site for her in the land where he is sojourning, the place that the Bible describes as "Kiriath-arba—now Hebron—in the land of Canaan" (Genesis 23:2).

After wailing over her and mourning her, he approaches a Hittite to ask permission to bury Sarah in that place, and to act as an agent to approach the owner of a piece of property that Abraham wishes to purchase as the gravesite. Abraham says:

> **Anochi-I** am a resident alien among you; sell me a burial site that I may remove my dead for burial. —Genesis 23:3

At this most painful time in his life, in his deep sadness, Abraham asks a favor from people he barely knows; Abraham speaks from the deepest part of his GodSelf, his **Anochi-I, God Within** because this is where his greatest God-like grace and compassion reside.

When Abraham seeks a wife for his son Isaac, he does not want Isaac to marry one of the local Canaanite women. Abraham senses that the covenant he has made with God must be continued through family lineage. He sends Eliezer, his steward, back to the ancestral homeland to find a wife for Isaac from his own family-tribe.

Abraham begins by charging Eliezer with his task.

> and I will make you swear . . . that you will not take a wife for my son from the daughters of the Canaanites among whom **Anochi-I** dwell. —Genesis 24:3

In the midst of the foreign community where he lives, Abraham's GodSelf is not comfortable, especially when it comes to finding a wife for his son.

Much of the exchange between the servant, the young woman he finds, and her family is in the voice of **Anochi-I**.

Eliezer says:

> Here **Anochi-I** stand by the spring as the daughters of the townsmen come to draw water. —Genesis 24:13

The woman identifies herself,

Anochi-I am the daughter of . . .   —GENESIS 24:24

The servant is overjoyed.

Anochi-I have been guided on my errand by YHWH. . . .
                                                —GENESIS 24:27

The young woman's brother offers hospitality,

Come in, O blessed of YHWH. Why do you remain outside when
Anochi-I have made ready the house, and a place for the camels?
                                                —GENESIS 24:31

To find love, to welcome love, to commit to love, and to affirm the covenant of love is not a simple human endeavor. The inspiration for human love comes directly from the pure love of God; human love is a reflection of God's perfect covenantal love. To seek and find the deepest, the most real human love means going to the **AnochiSelf**, to **God Within**.

Abraham knew that, and sent his servant on an **Anochi-I** mission. The servant went looking for love from the **Anochi-I** place in his being. The young woman, Rebecca, and her family embraced love from the **Anochi-I** within themSelves. Isaac and Rebecca lived their love, and assured the continuation of covenantal love with God, through the **Anochi-I, God Within**, of the depths of their beings.

Anochi, I-Source is the core of **Anochi-I** human love.

In a well-known passage of Torah, a very hungry Esau is about to sell his firstborn birthright to his twin brother Jacob for the price of a pot of porridge. Esau is a man of the fields, a hunter, providing for the material needs of the family. Jacob is a quiet man of home and spirit. And Esau said to Jacob, "Give me some of that red stuff [the porridge] to gulp down, for **Anochi-I** am famished. . . ." (Genesis 25:30).

Jacob said, "First sell me your birthright [of the firstborn]" (Genesis 25:31).

Esau said, "**Anochi-I** Am at the point of death, so of what use is the birthright to me?" (Genesis 25:32).

Esau realizes that his hunger is not just physical; it is spiritual. His inner sense of the Divine has withered and is about to dry up. He senses the errors of his ways in choosing a life of physical prowess over a life of the spirit. He is spiritually famished. He knows that his brother Jacob, who has chosen the spiritual life, is the rightful inheritor of the spiritual blessing of the birthright, so he is ready to concede it.

Yet, it is not so simple. Their father Isaac has high regard and love for Esau, because he is the firstborn. And, as was the custom in those days, the firstborn always gets the choicest blessing—no matter what deal his younger brother made with him. So, to receive the blessing of the firstborn—which is most important because it will be not just the blessing of material inheritance, but the blessing of spiritual inheritance—Jacob must deceive his father.

With the help of his mother, who plans and aids in the deception, Jacob puts animal skins on his arms so that his blind father will assume that he is Esau, the hairy one. He comes to his father, who asks, "Which of my sons are you?" (Genesis 27:18).

Jacob lies. He says to his father:

> **Anochi-I** am Esau your firstborn . . . Pray, sit and eat of my game [the food Esau had been instructed to kill and prepare as a meal for his father] that you may give me your innermost blessing.
> —GENESIS 27:19

Jacob speaks in the **Anochi-I, God Within** voice. But, he is speaking as if he were Esau. So, who is really speaking? Is it Jacob? Or is Jacob somehow expressing his inner sense that he knows it should be Esau standing before their father?

The answer becomes clear. Isaac—in a very well-known verse of Bible—says, "The voice is the voice of Jacob, but the hands are the hands of Esau" . . . so he blesses him (Genesis 27:22).

Isaac is still not quite convinced, so he asks one more time, "Are you really my son Esau?" And he [Jacob] said, "*Ani*—I am" (Genesis 27:24). At the moment of ultimate truth, Jacob responds with the *Ani*—the simple "I"—instead of the GodSelf, **Anochi-I, God Within**.

Isaac's suspicions are confirmed. Jacob reveals the deception through the language he uses—which Isaac certainly understands. So, why does Isaac proceed to give Jacob the blessing of the firstborn? Isaac is a willing unnamed co-conspirator for he knows, at the deepest level, that the spiritual blessing must go to Jacob, because the spiritual inheritance must continue. Jacob, far more than Esau, is the likely transmitter. So, the ruse—silently agreed upon—is complete, and the spiritual blessing winds up where it belongs.

Yet, all is not lost for Esau. With the food to revive him, he survives physically. He receives a fine material blessing from his father, which is rightly deserved and rightly placed.

Yet, because of this incident, Esau and Jacob become estranged. After high Torah drama, they eventually reconcile, each becoming the father of a great—but separate—nation.

The story of the twins is one of the Bible's poignant and painful sagas. To this very day, the hope of the world is that the descendants of Jacob and Esau—the modern-day Jews and Arabs—will remember and touch the **Anochi-I, Anochi Within**, restore the ancient blessings, and live with each other in peace.

Joseph, who is clearly his father's favorite son, angers his brothers by flaunting his specially decorated coat—commonly known as "the coat of many colors"—and by telling them the interpretation of his dreams that he will rule over them.

In order to alleviate the tension between Joseph and his brothers, their father Jacob sends his sons out to the pastures to shepherd the flocks. Not content to leave well-enough alone, Joseph follows them. A man comes across him wandering in the field, and asks Joseph what he is seeking. Joseph says:

Anochi-I Am looking for my brothers. . . .   —GENESIS 37:16

Is he still lording it over his brothers, claiming that he is better than they—that he is God-like in his being, and that they are less than he? Or, is he acknowledging the rising up of the God-like qualities of acceptance, understanding, compassion, and love that are within him?

From the text, the answer is not clear. Either way, the use of **Anochi-I** surely indicates Joseph is aware of his **Anochi-I, Anochi Within**, his GodSelf, and intends it to influence his behavior.

There is even deeper meaning, as well. Being aware of his **God Within** means that Joseph is already being Divinely guided. The "unnamed man" who sends Joseph in the direction of his brothers begins a series of events that is the Divine "blueprint" being played out in exact sequence. These step-by-step incidents—some of which happen for no apparent reason and have little logical explanation at the time—result in Joseph being sold into slavery in Egypt; being imprisoned; being released from prison to interpret the Pharaoh's dreams; being appointed chancellor over all of Egypt, and saving it from famine; Joseph's family coming to Egypt to be saved from starvation; Joseph's family prospering, and growing large and strong; the enslavement of his descendants; the redemption of the slaves from Egypt; the revelation of the Ten Commandments at Sinai; the trek through the desert; and the eventual entrance into the Promised Land.

It is in this way that Joseph triggers the key event in Jewish history—the making of the Hebrews into a nation; and one of the core moments of human history—the theophany at Sinai, which gives God's word and will to the world. All this from the first recognition of his **Anochi-I**, his **God Within**.

What marvels await each and every one of us—and our world with us—when we find our own **Anochi-I, God Within**?

After being with his son Joseph in Egypt for seventeen years, Jacob is about to die at the age of 147. Jacob's wish is that he not be buried in Egypt, but that his remains be returned to the family burial plot in Hebron. He says to Joseph:

> When I lie down with my fathers [meaning: when I die] take me up
> from Egypt and bury me in their burial place. He [Joseph] replied,
> "**Anochi-I** will do as you have spoken."   —GENESIS 47:30

Joseph does not promise to fulfill his father's wishes lightly or casually. He reaches to the GodSelf within him, to demonstrate the depth and the sincerity of his promise.

When the plagues are being brought upon Egypt, there is an extraordinary use of **Anochi-I** coming from the mouth of a human being—Pharaoh.

Three plagues—the Nile turning to blood, frogs, and lice—have already overrun Egypt. Pharaoh's magicians acknowledge that this is much more than the kind of magic they can produce. They concede, saying, "This is the finger of *Elohim* [God's representative on Earth, who, at that time, was YHWH]" (Exodus 8:15).

But, Pharaoh will still not let the Hebrew slaves go. So, the fourth plague—swarms of insects—comes. Pharaoh is overwhelmed; now he seems ready to partially relent. Pharaoh says,

> **Anochi-I** will let you go to sacrifice in the wilderness to YHWH,
> who is in the office of your *Elohim;* but do not go very far. Plead
> for me.   —EXODUS 8:24

What an amazing statement!

The plagues have had an effect on Pharaoh's hard heart. He recognizes the power of **Anochi**, who is Source, represented by YHWH. He even asks Moses to intervene with the Hebrew God for him. Pharaoh has been touched by **Anochi**, and recognizes his own GodSelf, **God Within**. The embrace of that **Anochi-I** is what causes his heart to soften a bit.

Moses responds to this softening of Pharaoh's heart through his own **Anochi-I**.

He says to Pharaoh:

> When **Anochi-I** leave your presence, I will plead with YHWH that
> the swarms of insects depart . . . —EXODUS 8:25

Sadly, the **Anochi** influence within Pharaoh is short-lived, and
he quickly returns to his hard-hearted, stubborn, authoritarian ways.
However, for a brief moment, even in the midst of perpetuating evil,
Pharaoh feels his **Anochi-I, God Within**, and feels the power the
Anochi-I of Moses that evokes his reply.

During the trek in the desert, the freed slaves complain about lack of
water and, particularly, about having no meat to eat. Moses is overwhelmed by their harsh words and rebellious attitude. He says:

> **Anochi-I** cannot carry this whole people by myself; it is too much
> for me. —NUMBERS 11:14

Burdened by his task, and overcome by the behavior—and the obvi-
ous ingratitude—of the very people to whom he has given so much,
Moses says to God that even **God Within** me cannot handle this ordeal.

Moses acknowledges that as great as it is, his **Anochi-I, God
Within**, is limited. Even though he has often channeled **Anochi,
I-Source**, he, Moses, understands that he is not God; he is a human
being with all the human foibles, flaws, and failings.

By admitting, even reluctantly, that he is not able to handle his
responsibility—massive though it is—Moses begins to feel the heavy
toll on his human emotion, and will begin to experience the severe consequences that result.

After redeeming the Hebrew slaves; bringing them to Sinai to receive
the law; trekking for forty years through the desert, facing all the hard-
ships of the journey; enduring the almost constant complaints of the
people; fighting fierce military battles against numerous enemies; and
realizing that he will not enter the promised land, Moses is about to die.

He says to the people:

Anochi-I Am now one hundred twenty years old. I can no longer be active. Moreover, YHWH has said to me, "You shall not cross over the Jordan." —DEUTERONOMY 31:2

Moses is exhausted: physically, emotionally, and—most of all—spiritually. His **Anochi-I, God Within** can no longer face the challenges or carry the burdens of leading the people. He is ready to give up leadership.

The Midrash teaches that he is still feisty enough to argue with **Anochi** that he should be permitted to enter the Promised Land, if only as a cow, if only as a bird. However, that is not to be.

Moses dies and his **Anochi-I, God Within** returns to its Maker, to **Anochi-I, Source**, the transcendent God of the Heavens, where Moses receives eternal reward for his service on Earth.

WHERE **ANOCHI** IS NOT

The word **Anochi** does not appear even once in the biblical book of Leviticus. This makes sense, since Leviticus is also known as *Torat Kohanim,* the "Torah [law/instruction] of the Priests." It is in Leviticus that the priests establish their authority to represent the people in the worship of God.

With our new understanding, we know that **Anochi** has put YHWH into the office of *Elohim* to serve as **Anochi's** deputy, as God on Earth. To establish YHWH's place and authority, the priests are given—and take even more upon themselves—the exclusive role of serving YHWH.

Leviticus is filled with hundreds of details of priestly dress and behavior, the form and accoutrements of the Sanctuary, the modes and methods of sacrificial worship, and all the other minute instructions for priestly function and worship of YHWH.

The entire book of Leviticus focuses on the primacy of YHWH; the role of the priests in representing and serving YHWH, and acclaiming and aggrandizing YHWH to the people; so it is understandable that the name **Anochi** does not appear in Leviticus.

Yet, even with this awareness, there is one verse in Leviticus that cries out for the name **Anochi**—where we hope, and even expect, that **Anochi's** name will appear. But, it is not there.

In what has come to be known as the "Holiness Code," YHWH speaks to Moses, instructing him to tell the whole community of the Israelites: "You shall be holy, for I, YHWH *Elohechem* [YHWH who is in the office of your *Elohim*—God on Earth] Am holy" (Leviticus 19:2).

Given all we have discovered, it would make perfect sense for the "I" spoken here to be the word **Anochi**—**Anochi, I-Source**. But, it is not. It is the common and simple *Ani,* the first person singular word for "I."

Even though **Anochi** is absent in all of Leviticus, for this one injunction—this singularly important instruction to imitate God by being holy—it would have been understandable for **Anochi** to insert **AnochiSelf**. It seems as if it would have been an even more powerful teaching if **Anochi, I-Source**, the whole, complete Source, had given it.

But, **Anochi** purposely did not intervene. YHWH speaks the words, using the common "I."

Why?

Since the purpose of the Book of Leviticus serves to establish the primacy of YHWH, **Anochi** did not want to do anything—to insert **AnochiSelf** at any place or any time—that would undermine the primacy of YHWH in the role of Earthly God.

It is as if the Chief Executive Officer of a company says, "I have appointed a Chief Operating Officer to deal with all the issues concerning the day-to-day running of our company. I will leave all decisions—especially those about relationships with vendors, employees, and customers—to the COO. For the ultimate good of the company, I will not interfere with the business operations, so that the COO and all those she works with can bond together and establish a full, trusting relationship. I will do nothing to undermine the authority of the COO."

So, as much as **Anochi** may have wanted to give this instruction of holiness—and as much as we might want to hear it directly from **Anochi**—we understand **Anochi's** decision to withhold **AnochiSelf** from the time and place when YHWH's authority and relationship with the people Israel had to be firmly established.

THE DOUBLE "I": MYSTERY SOLVED

Perhaps the most well-known—and least understood—use of the word **Anochi** in Torah is in the story of Jacob when he is fleeing from what he assumes is the wrath of his brother whom he had deceived for the blessing of the birthright (Genesis 28:10–22).

Jacob stops for the night, and in his sleep he dreams of a ladder to Heaven.

> Behold, angels of *Elohim* were going up and down [the ladder].
> —GENESIS 28:12
>
> And, then, the very next sentence says: "And YHWH, who was standing beside him, said, 'I Am YHWH. . . .'"   —GENESIS 28:13

This is one of those confusing early Book of Genesis stories where God is called both *Elohim* and YHWH, often in successive sentences, and sometimes in the same sentence.

Modern biblical scholarship suggests that the presence of these two names of God back to back indicate that two similar oral-tradition tribal stories were woven together into one story in the written version that has come down to us. We know that there is a deeper explanation—hidden until now.

For, immediately, Jacob hears:

> *"V'hinei, Anochi i'mach . . ."* Commonly translated: "Behold, I Am with you (and will protect you wherever you go, and bring you back to this land)."

Now we know. It is neither *Elohim* nor YHWH speaking. It is **Anochi, I-Source.**

We translate:

> **Anochi, I-Source** Am with you . . .   —GENESIS 28:15

Why is this one of those times when the circumstances are

important enough for **Anochi** to insert **AnochiSelf** into the situation?

Jacob is worried that the God of his father and grandfather is just a neighborhood god, like all the other gods in the area. So, **Anochi, AnochiSelf**, assures Jacob that **Anochi, I-Source** is the One universal God, who is everywhere, and will be with him wherever he goes.

Jacob is amazed and grateful for this revelation:

And Jacob awoke from his sleep, and he said, *"achen, yesh* YHWH *bamakom hazeh, v'***Anochi** *lo yadati."*

In the commonly accepted translation:

Surely, YHWH is in this place and I, I did not know it.

—GENESIS 28:16

The troubling difficulty in this sentence is Jacob's double use of the word "I." "I, I did not know." "I did not know" is conveyed through the Hebrew words, *lo yadati*. In the common translation that assumes the word **Anochi** simply means "I," the presence of the word **Anochi** is completely superfluous. But it is there, so it results in the reading of the double "I." "I, I did not know."

This double use of the word "I" has puzzled commentators throughout the generations. Recently, modern spiritual theologian Rabbi Lawrence Kushner wrote a book entitled, *God Was in This Place & I, I Did Not Know*, where he gathered together the interpretations of this verse from sages through the centuries, and added his own modern spiritual commentary.

None of the commentators ever offered a definitive answer. The question of the double "I" remains a riddle—until now. For now, with our new understanding of the real name of God, we can retranslate and finally make sense of this verse.

Because this is such a unique use of the word **Anochi**—resulting in the double "I"—this verse has a singular translation, used nowhere else in Torah.

Rather than **Anochi** being spoken in the voice of God or in the voice of a human being, here a human being is referring to God as **Anochi**.

> Surely, YHWH is in this place [occupying the office of God on Earth—*Elohim*], but *lo yadati,* I did not know [meaning: I was not aware of] **Anochi**.

Until this moment, Jacob knew only aspects of God—panels of the Divine Beach Ball. He did not know—or even know about—the whole, full God, **Anochi**. In his dream, he is told: *"Anochi i'mach,"*—*"***Anochi***, I-Source** Am with you." He is introduced to the whole, full, complete God—**Anochi**.

First, he is amazed: *lo yadati,* I never knew; I was never aware of **Anochi**.

The Zohar (*Vayetse* 1:150b) equates **Anochi** with *Shechinah,* the Divine Feminine. "Has all this been revealed to me, and yet I have not endeavored to know **Anochi**, entering under the wings of *Shechinah,* becoming complete?" This mystical tradition perfectly delineates that the whole God—the God Jacob seeks and to whom he is being introduced— is everything, a full union of the Divine Masculine and Feminine.

Awareness hits Jacob; his consciousness is raised; he understands. **Anochi** is not just a neighborhood god. **Anochi** is the full, whole God. **Anochi** is everywhere. **Anochi** will be with him wherever he goes.

In his awe and gratitude, Jacob shouts out:

> How awesome is this place!

He continues,

> *Ki im beit Elohim.* It is the house of *Elohim.* . . . this [place] is the gateway to Heaven. —GENESIS 28:17

Jacob intuitively knows that, at this fleeting moment, **Anochi, I-Source** has put **AnochiSelf** into the office of *Elohim* to teach an eternal lesson: **Anochi** is God. **Anochi** is God of everyone and everywhere. **Anochi** is God everlasting.

And this place, where **Anochi** has revealed **AnochiSelf**, is a "gateway to Heaven," a place where Heaven and Earth—and thus, God and humankind—have met and touched.

Having met **Anochi, I-Source,** Jacob is able to sense a bit of his own GodSelf, a bit of **Anochi-I,** his **God Within.** In response to this awesome outer and inner revelation, Jacob makes a vow, saying,

> If *Elohim* is with me, and protects me on this journey that **Anochi-I** am making, and gives me bread to eat and clothing to wear, and if I return safely to my father's house, then YHWH will be my God.
> —GENESIS 28:20–21

Even grasping that **Anochi, I-Source** has put **AnochiSelf** into the office of *Elohim* to teach the lesson of universality, and even accepting that YHWH is the deputy who will manifest as God during his travels, Jacob's own **Anochi-I, God Within** is still unsure enough—and bold and brazen enough—to make his acceptance of **Anochi** through YHWH conditional. In essence, he says, "*If* You do this for me, *then* I will accept You as my God."

Poor **Anochi!** It is not easy being God! Even with this incredible display of Holy Presence, Jacob still does not fully, faithfully embrace; Jacob still demands more proof.

Yet, we need not worry. For, with our modern perspective on this age-old story, we know that this is a seminal moment in the human evolution of opening to the real name of God, and thus coming to know the real God, the God of all time and space.

Because we now know the real identity of **Anochi, I-Source,** the real name of God, the millennia-old problem of the double "I" is solved.

THE REST OF THE STORY

Jacob travels to Haran. He is taken in by his uncle Laban, and marries both Laban's daughters, Leah and Rachel. He also consorts with their handmaids, Bilhah and Zilpah, and fathers eleven sons and one daughter. (A twelfth son will be born to him later.)

After fourteen years of service—despite the reality of having to face his deceived brother Esau when he returns home—Jacob is ready to leave. However, Laban is reluctant to let him go because Jacob had served him well, built up his fortunes—and, besides, he would be taking the daughters and grandchildren with him!

When Laban objects to Jacob's plan to leave, Jacob counters by saying, "I have served you well, and your livestock has fared [well] with me" (Genesis 30:29).

> For the little you had before I came has grown to much, since YHWH blessed you wherever I turned. And now, when can **Anochi-I** make provision for my own household? —GENESIS 30:30

Not only is Jacob saying that he wants to work for himself, in order to achieve his own material gain, but he is saying that the only way he can really become a man is to no longer be under the protection of his uncle/father-in-law's household. He must assume responsibility for his own spiritual growth. His primary reason for leaving is so that he can come into his own **Anochi-I, God Within,** his own GodSelf.

Six years later—after very convoluted negotiations about how Jacob would be compensated for his work, and after unpleasantries and deceptions, large and small, on both sides—Jacob knows that it is time for him to leave. He says to Laban's sons:

> **Anochi-I** see that your father's manner toward me is not as it has been in the past. But *Elohim* [the God who is in the office of God on Earth] of my father has been with me.   —GENESIS 31:5

Later, Jacob defends his service to Laban himself.

> These twenty years **Anochi-I** have spent in your service, your ewes and she-goats never miscarried, nor did I feast on the rams of your flock. That which was torn by beasts I never brought to you. **Anochi-I** made good the loss; you exacted it of me, whether snatched by day or by night.   —GENESIS 31:38–39

Jacob's **Anochi-I, God Within** is confident that he has dealt fairly and generously with his uncle/father-in-law. His sense of self is firm and unwavering, because he knows that he is deeply in touch with his GodSelf, from which he derives a calm and untroubled soul.

Ready to leave, Jacob receives a much-welcome assurance from **Anochi, I-Source.**

> **Anochi, I-Source** Am the God of Beth El, where you anointed a pillar, and where you made a vow to Me. Now, arise and leave this land and return to your native land. —GENESIS 31:1

There are just two adventures left in this saga. Returning home, Jacob must face his brother Esau, whom he deceived for the blessing of the firstborn.

He sends messengers and gifts to his brother; he separates the family so that if Esau attacks, only part of Jacob's family will be in danger. Then, from the depth of his GodSelf, he prays:

> Please deliver me from the hand of my brother Esau, because **Anochi-I** Am afraid that he will come and strike me down, mothers and children alike. —GENESIS 32:12

Making this fervent plea, Jacob then spends the night alone, where he wrestles with (choose one or more): God, an angel of God, a man, himself, his twinness, his conscience, his soul.

In the morning, Jacob has prevailed. His name is changed to *Yisrael*—Israel, meaning the one who "wrestles with God." Unafraid, filled with confidence and with a true sense of his **Anochi-I, God Within** GodSelf, he meets his brother; they reconcile, and travel back to the family home, where Jacob reunites with his parents. His father— on his deathbed twenty years before—is miraculously still alive.

What more could Jacob ask? Everything he sought has been fulfilled. His initial dream-question was, "Will this **Anochi** be with me and protect me wherever I go?" Clearly, the answer is yes.

Anochi accompanied Jacob on his journey. **Anochi** protected Jacob through all the twenty years of his sojourn. **Anochi** accompanied Jacob on his return home. And **Anochi** protected him from any harm his brother Esau might bring.

Anochi has surely proven **AnochiSelf** as a universal God of guidance and protection.

Many years later, when Jacob is an old man, he is told that his beloved son Joseph is still alive and is the chancellor over all of Egypt. Jacob wants to go to be with him, but he is unsure and afraid of what lies ahead in the journey and in the reunion.

Once again, **Anochi** offers assurance.

> And [**Anochi**] said, "**Anochi, I-Source** Am the God of your father. Do not fear to go down to Egypt. **Anochi, I-Source** will go down to Egypt with you, and **Anochi, I-Source** will bring you back. . . ."
> —GENESIS 46:3–4

The "travel texts" have served their purpose. The question is clearly answered. **Anochi, I-Source**, the full essence of Source, is the universal God—the God for all time, all place, and all people.

THE ODDEST **ANOCHI** OF ALL

In one of the Bible's most difficult and fascinating stories, **Anochi** appears in the oddest of all voices.

Chapter 22 of the Book of Numbers reports that the Israelites have just won military victory over the Amorites, a fierce desert tribe that had tried to destroy them.

The Moabites, a neighboring tribe—joined by another neighbor, the Midianites—are afraid that the Israelites, on their single-minded journey to the Promised Land, will destroy them too.

Balak, the king of Moab, sends messengers to Balaam, a highly able and powerful desert prophet, well-known for his cultic skills: "Whomever you bless is blessed, and whomever you curse is accursed" (Numbers 22:6).

Balak's request to Balaam is simple:

Please come and curse this people [the Israelites] for me, for it is too powerful for me; perhaps I will be able to strike it and drive it away from the land. —NUMBERS 22:6

Balaam—finely attuned and "equal opportunity" prophet that he is—knows that YHWH was the God of the Israelites, so he consults with YHWH, asking if he should fulfill the request to curse. YHWH's response is "No," so Balaam sends the messengers away.

The king, not about to take "No" for an answer, repeatedly sends messengers to Balaam, but the answer is always the same—"No, I will not curse this people—not for all the riches of your kingdom."

Then in a most curious reversal, YHWH gives Balaam permission to go to curse the Israelites. Throughout the ages, the biblical commentators have tried to understand this very strange transposition. Some speculate that because of Balaam's well-known greed, he would have eventually succumbed to the entreaties; some suggest that YHWH is permitting the enemies to be built up before they were destroyed; some posit that YHWH decides not to interfere with human free will. All the speculation is just that; the biblical text does not indicate a reason for YHWH's unexpected change of instruction. Whatever the reason, Balaam takes advantage of what he perceived to be YHWH's permission, and goes to curse the Israelites.

Balaam sets out on the journey, riding the donkey that he has ridden all his life. Three times, an angel of YHWH appears to impede the journey; Balaam does not see the angel, but the donkey does! Each time, the donkey turns away from continuing on the journey: once into a field; once against a wall; once into a very narrow place. Balaam, still blind to the angel, strikes the donkey to turn her back to the road.

After the third time that Balaam ignores the donkey, she turns to him and says:

"Look, Am **Anochi-I** not the donkey you have been riding all along until this day? Have I been in the habit of doing this to you?" And he answered, "No."   —NUMBERS 22:30

A talking donkey!

A talking donkey who speaks in the voice of **Anochi-I, God Within**!

How can this be?

The echoes of Egypt are loud. Like Pharaoh's, Balaam's heart has been hardened. As in Egypt, YHWH has sent messages that are repeatedly ignored. The third time, the donkey goes to a *makom tzar,* a narrow place, a word that may be related to *Mitzrayim,* the narrow place that was Egypt. Still, Balaam's heart is hardened and he does not pay attention or relent.

Balaam does not comprehend, but a donkey does.

Animals are pure and innocent; they do not have egos or small selves. They have only GodSelves; they are filled with love. So, the donkey can only speak from her **Anochi-I, God Within**.

The donkey "miraculously" reminds Balaam that he has forgotten or ignored his **Anochi-I, God Within**. For, if he were consciously aware of his **God Within**, then even with God's perceived permission—he could not be on a journey to curse God's people.

Awareness begins to dawn. YHWH opens Balaam's eyes, and he sees the angel.

The angel scolds him:

Why have you beaten your donkey these three times? It is **Anochi, I-Source's** [messenger/representative] who came out to impede you, for you hastened on the road to oppose Me.   —NUMBERS 22:32

Anochi, I-Source, through the angel-messenger, tells Balaam that he has done wrong. He had been warned all along, but his hardened heart could not hear or see.

Now he understands. He agrees to speak only what God tells him to speak.

He continues his journey, but telling Balak that he will speak only whatever YHWH, who is in the office of *Elohim,* tells him to speak.

When Balaam reaches the summit above the camp of the Israelites, he has Balak set up altars for prayer. And, Balaam finally understands. He says to Balak:

> Stay here next to your offerings, while **Anochi-I** seek a manifestation [a message from God] over there.   —NUMBERS 23:15

The message from God comes in a parable that ultimately results in Balaam not cursing the Israelites, but blessing them instead. His blessing is so beautiful and sublime that it eventually becomes the opening prayer of the morning synagogue worship service:

> How goodly are your tents, O Jacob, your dwelling places, O Israel.
>   —NUMBERS 24:5

What a story!

Curses. Blessings. Divinations. A talking donkey. Conversations with God. An angelic messenger. High drama. A "storybook" ending, where they all live happily ever after.

What happened here? What are we supposed to learn?

Balaam has finally touched his **Anochi-I**, his **God Within**, and his GodSelf leads him not to evil, but to good.

This oddest of all **Anochi** texts is a lesson for the ages: **Anochi, I-Source** awaits—and expects—our awareness of our **Anochi-I, God Within**, so that we can bring God-like goodness and **Anochi's** blessings to our world.

To read a sampling of **Anochi** texts in the second and third sections of the Bible—Prophets and Writings—please see appendix I.

SEEK AND YE SHALL FIND

—————◄○►—————

A mother and father were looking out the window of their house, watching their young daughter play in the backyard.

They saw her stand in the middle of the yard, and then run to stand behind a tree, or crouch under a bush, or kneel beside a corner of the house.

After a minute or two she threw her arms up over her head, clapped her hands, and—cheering happily—she skipped back to the center of the yard.

She stood there for a few moments, and then began to count out loud, "One, two, three, four, five, six, seven, eight, nine, ten! Ready or not, here I come."

She ran and looked behind a tree, or under a bush, or in a flower bed, or around the corner of the house.

Before long, she again threw her arms up over her head, clapped her hands, and—cheering happily—she skipped back to the center of the yard.

Then she picked up a ball, tossed it up in the air, caught it, and tossed it up again and again.

Smiling widely, she set down the ball, and began the game all over again.

Very curious as to what she was doing, her parents came out to the yard, and asked, "What game are you playing?"

She said, "I'm playing hide-and-seek. And, I'm playing catch."

"But," said her father, "You need at least two people to play hide-and-seek and catch. I don't see any other children here. How are you playing hide-and-seek and catch by yourself?"

"I'm not playing by myself," she said. "I'm playing with God."

"Playing with God?" her mother said, in great wonder. "How do you do that?"

"It's simple," said, the little girl. "I hide and God finds me. Then, God hides, and I find God."

"And then, God and I play catch. I throw the ball up to God, and God catches it. Then God throws the ball to me, and I catch it."

—◄○►—

The Sage teaches:

"Where is God? God is everywhere you let God in."[1]

SIX

ANOCHI AND US

What does it mean to have found **Anochi**?

Is this merely an academic exercise, over which scholars will debate issues of history, language, etymology, and theology?

Is it religious blasphemy that will upset long-held comfortable beliefs and behaviors?

Or, is it long-hidden truth that has been waiting, waiting for the right moment to reveal itself, so that we can finally know and embrace the wholeness, the totality, the full essence of God; the God who is the Everything of Everything, the Oneness of all that is?

> *The master, who had been banished from his country was asked,*
> *"Do you ever feel nostalgia for your homeland?"*
> *"No," he replied.*
> *"But," protested one of his disciples, "how can you not miss*
> *your home?"*
> *The master replied, "You cease to be in exile, when you realize that*
> *God is your Home."*

At this very moment in time, we become the most fortunate generation to live on Earth since the Garden of Eden.

For, now, we have found and can meet **Anochi**.

We have found our Home.

For all their worth, religions—with their theologies, texts, rituals, observances, traditions, and communities—are mere pathways. The true quest of the spiritual journey is to know God, to be with God.

We now see in the Bible the clear presence of the transcendent and the immanent God—both the **Anochi Above** and the **Anochi Within**—**Anochi** who is both so far and so near, so powerful and so loving; **Anochi** who is the Eternity of the Universe, and at the very same time, the nurturing, InDwelling Presence.

Knowing **Anochi**, knowing God's true identity, means that we can now come to know the fullness of Source, the wholeness of God. We can come closer and closer to knowing the real essence of God's Being, and of our relationship with the Divine.

- It means that we know that **Anochi** is in no way delimited; that the God we meet in the Bible is only aspects of **Anochi**—individual panels of the Divine Beach Ball.

  We no longer have to relate solely to a deputy God; we never again have to wonder about the biblical accounts of God's behavior. We now know that the angry, vengeful God of Torah is just an aspect of Source. We can finally put that biblical God into context and perspective.

- It means that we no longer have to settle for the male, hierarchical image of God, and the predominately masculine language and names for God.

  We can know **Anochi** who is everything—male and female, all in One—no duality, no separation; whole and complete.

  And, we who are created in the image of **Anochi** can reflect **Anochi**. We can reach into the archetypes that reside within each of us: men look to their feminine archetypes and find compassion; women in their masculine archetypes find strength.

  On Earth, the eternal "battle of the sexes" can end. For we know that as is God, we are One.

- Knowing **Anochi** means knowing that God is all around you, and within you, and gives you life.

There was once a baby fish who swam up to his mother and asked,

   "Mom, what is this water that I hear so much about?"

   His mother said, "Silly guppy, water is all around you, and within you,
and gives you life. If you want to know what water is, swim to the top of
the pond and lie there for a while. Then you will find out what water is."

   There was once a little bear cub who walked over to her mother and
asked, "Mom, what is this air I hear so much about?"

   Her mother said, "Silly little bear, air is all around you, and within
you, and gives you life. If you want to know what air is, just stick your head
in the stream. Then you will find out what air is."

   There was once a young man who came to his parents, and said,
"Mom, Dad, what is this God I hear so much about?"

Anochi is the eternal Creator and Sustainer of the vastness of the universe. **Anochi** is the sweet, gentle, holy Presence within you, calling you to your God-ness and your greatness.

- It means that **Anochi** loves every child of the universe, every soul in human body. Regardless of what each person, each group, each faith community, chooses to call the Divine Parent, **Anochi** is **Anochi**.

  We can rid ourSelves of our sibling rivalries, our competitions, our conflicts, our desire to think that our Father/Mother God loves us best.

  We are all One, and **Anochi** loves us all.

- Above all, knowing **Anochi** means knowing that God is Love— pure, total, unequivocal, unconditional, absolute, eternal Love. Knowing **Anochi** is knowing Love, being held in Love, being Love.

As the French author Laurence Cossé explains in her intriguing book, *A Corner of the Veil,*

With the world, God created totality of being. Everything that is has no other meaning but being . . . What is, is nothing else but

God in the process of being. We are grounded in God, each person for what he is.[1]

> Anochi's *Being is Love.*
> All creation—and, surely, each and every human
>   being—is Love.
> For all this and more, we come to be with **Anochi.**

YOU ARE **ANOCHI'S** PROPHET

The Word Is in You

*And they heard the Voice . . . a great Voice
that never ceases . . .* —GENESIS 3:8, DEUTERONOMY 5:19

Biblical times were characterized by the ever-present possibility of individual prophecy—the notion that God could and would reveal God's Divine will to any person at any time.

Later (in a time we now call "The Rabbinic Period," beginning around 200 BCE) the sages effectively cut off individual prophecy by claiming that God's continuing revelation could come only through them, and that they alone would receive and transmit God's word. This scholar-centered, law-based religion is still practiced as mainstream Judaism to this very day.

Christianity came along and, at its core, taught that the relationship with God does not depend primarily on law, but can come through faith and love. Later, Islam was an attempt to synthesize the sometimes competing natures of law and spirit.

Today, there are those of all faiths who meticulously adhere to the laws of their religions and communities. Many however, while still embracing ethical and moral laws, consider ritual law informative, instructive, and (perhaps) inspirational—but not binding.

Slowly, yet profoundly, a new religious sensibility is emerging, leading to a new era of religious thought and practice. This new era is still characterized by deep commitment to the communal covenant with **Anochi** and to being part of sacred community. Yet, its primacy is the return to the very real notion that each person—each individual human soul—can have a deep, personal, intimate relationship with **Anochi**; to hear directly from **Anochi**, and to talk directly to **Anochi**.

In my book, *Soul Judaism* (*Dancing with God*, in its original hardcover publication), I term this new era "Neshamah-Soul-Judaism," because it is centered in the soul-to-soul relationship between **Anochi** and each and every person—you.

No less than Moses, or Jeremiah, or Elijah—and, depending on your belief system, Jesus or Mohammed—you are a prophet. As **Anochi** came to them, **Anochi** comes to you.

According to the Bible, the prophet Ezekiel had an amazing vision of a gleaming *merkavah*—a chariot—drawn by mythic winged beasts that brought him the mission of his prophecy (Ezekiel 1).

Now that we have found **Anochi**, you can receive your *merkavah* to meet **Anochi, I-Source**, the God of the Heavens, and **Anochi-I, God Within**.

Anochi's messages will come to you when you are with **Anochi** in the quiet of prayer and meditation—and in every place, in every moment, in the "rough and tumble" arena of life.

Here is a little prayer that you can say, asking **Anochi** to elevate your gift of prophecy.

Anochi,
Please:
Attune my hearing,
so that You can speak to me.
Sharpen my seeing,
so that You can show me.
Hone my senses,
so that You can dream into me by day and by night.
Let me be ever-open and ever-ready,
so that You can inspirit me.

Let me be a channel,
so that You can flow through me.

WD

CONNECTING WITH **ANOCHI**

Personal, Intimate Encounters

If we wish to begin to relate to **Anochi**, the Oneness of God, then we can meet **Anochi**, as did Moses.

Standing at the Burning Bush, Moses met **Anochi**, and began the relationship that led to the freedom of redemption and the revelation of God's word at Sinai. The intimate encounter set the path toward the communal covenant that, for all its cosmic significance, always remains enwrapped in the personal connection.

You, too, can meet **Anochi** when you stand at your own Burning Bush.

You might begin the conversation with this little prayer:

The Bush burns.
The Gates are open.
I Am here.

Anochi,
Source of all Worlds,
Breath of all Life,
Oneness of all Being:

I open my heart to Your Holy Presence.
I open my soul to Your Enveloping Voice.

Be with me.
Embrace me.
Hear me.
Answer me.

Please, answer me,
on this day when I call.

Guide me.
Challenge me.
Inspirit me.
Bless me.

Hold me in Your great compassion,
and keep me in Your saving truth.

WD & ELKD[2]

We can each form a deep, personal, intimate relationship with **Anochi**—a relationship with the God of love—by praying and meditating, by seeking new words and renewing mystical formulas, by daydreaming and night-dreaming, and in so many more spirit-filled ways. These pathways enable us to invoke, connect, and communicate with **Anochi**.

We can come to **Anochi** with quiet meditative chant.

And we can come to **Anochi** with joyous, rhythmic chant.

To hear these Anochi chants, please visit the website
www.GodisAnochi.com

And we can come to **Anochi** by listening to that still small voice, the sweet whispers, and even the "sounds of silence."

The journey begins deep inside yourself where you affirm the marvelous declaration of the biblical psalmist that **Anochi** is God.

In a unique text, **Anochi, AnochiSelf**, is in the office of *Elohim,* God on Earth, and says,

*"Harpu u-d'u ki **Anochi** Elohim,"* commonly translated as, "Be still and know that I Am God" (Psalms 46:11).

We now know that this verse means, "Be still and know that **Anochi** is [in the office of] *Elohim.*"

Or better, "Be still and know that **Anochi** is God."

Anochi says to us: "To know Me, you cannot know just an aspect, a part, of Me. You must know the Whole Me. So, right now, I place My **Anochi-Self** into the office of *Elohim,* so that I will be here as God on Earth. And, then, if you really, really want to know Me, you can.

"The way to know Me is to be still; quiet your mind from all extraneous chatter; focus; pay attention; be fully open; go to the deepest place within yourself, and you will find Me.

"There call to Me, call to **Anochi, I-Source**, and call to your GodSelf, to your **Anochi-I**. And you will know God.

"Then, talk, talk, talk, and I will hear you.

"Then listen, listen, listen, and you will know My plan for you; you will have glimpses of the answers to the mysteries of the universe; you will feel the unfolding of the desires of your heart; you will know your purpose and your mission; you will find the Oneness of God, and touch the God-ness of you.

"Like looking in a mirror, you will see and hear Me, and you will reflectively see and hear yourself—**Anochi-I**, your GodSelf."

When we are still, all is available. To help you call to **Anochi**, the fullness of God on Earth, you can sing this verse (Psalms 46:11), *"Harpu u-d'u ki Anochi Elohim."* "Be still and know that **Anochi** is God."

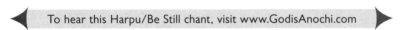
To hear this Harpu/Be Still chant, visit www.GodisAnochi.com

Now, to joyously celebrate your awareness and affirmation that **Anochi** is God, that **Anochi** is your God, and that **Anochi** is the God of All, you can chant the declaration, *Anochi Elohim,* "**Anochi** is God."

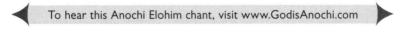
To hear this Anochi Elohim chant, visit www.GodisAnochi.com

We do not even have to use words to come to **Anochi**, or to be in **Anochi** connection. We can look at **Anochi's** name on the page: when we see the image of the Name, it is possible for us to imprint **Anochi's** Name into our psyches and our souls.

Look.
Take in the image.
Be in the Name.
Connect.

Anochi

I

Anochi *is* everything and everywhere. **Anochi** surrounds us and envelops us. We need only be conscious and aware enough to turn one way or the other to encounter **Anochi**, and to be with **Anochi**.

To remember to be with **Anochi**, you can chant this verse adapted from the Psalms (16:8), "*Shiviti Anochi L'negdi Tamid.*" "I place **Anochi** All-Ways before me."

To hear this Shiviti chant, visit www.GodisAnochi.com

ACKNOWLEDGING **ANOCHI**

Praising and Thanking the Whole **Anochi**

Knowing the wholeness of **Anochi** gives us a new way to relate to **Anochi**.

A personal confession: I love God. I have a deep, intimate relationship with God. I talk to God all the time.

But, for a long time now—even though it is deep in my tradition—I have been very uncomfortable with the Jewish prayer formula.

The rubric of the prayer-blessing begins:

"Blessed are You, YHWH-*Adonai, Elohenu,"*

translated as "Lord our God, King of the world." This is followed by praise and thanks for God's bounty and so many other of God's favors:

"who creates the fruit of the vine."
"who brings forth bread from the Earth."
"who keeps us in life, sustains us, and brings us to this moment."

While I am grateful for all these gifts, and wish to acknowledge and thank God for them—and while I am cognizant of the religious sage-centered world and sensibilities out of which these blessings grew—I am uncomfortable with a formula that addresses God as YHWH and "King," for this identifies God as exclusively male, and invokes His hierarchical and authoritarian attributes.

Furthermore, when the blessing praises God for giving commandments that are to be observed, added to the first words of the rubric are,

"who sanctified us through His commandments and commanded us . . ."

"to light the Sabbath candles."
"to light the Chanukah candles."
"to hear the sound of the shofar."

. . . and many more *mitzvot* (commands).

Again, I am uncomfortable with the image of a male God who commands, and whose means of making us holy is through the strict observance of directives and injunctions.

In this blessing formula, where is the God of love, the God of compassion, the God of gentle guidance?

Now, knowing the real name of God, knowing that **Anochi** is the wholeness, the totality, of all, we no longer need prayers or blessings that focus mainly on God's mighty power. Instead, we can formulate a new way to come to **Anochi** in prayer and blessing, celebrating the fullness, the Oneness—and surely, the love—of **Anochi**.

In my Jewish tradition, we can now say:

ברוך האָנֹכִי מקור כל העֹלָמֹות ורוח כל חי

Baruch *HaAnochi, M'kor kol ha-olamot, v'Ruach kol chai*

"Blessed is (the) Anochi—Source of all worlds, and Breath/Spirit of all life . . ."

This is the God I know, revere, and love. This is **Anochi!**

The "*Ha*" (before the name **Anochi**) in simple Hebrew means "the." The designation **THE Anochi** is used in this blessing to avoid confusion with dualism, or any interpretation that I—as a human being—am God, as opposed to having God within me. I Am of God, but I Am not God. Let there be no doubt: **Anochi** is One.

Thus, in this blessing, we are addressing the One and Only God— **THE Anochi**.

The second part of the blessing formula can now say:

אשר קדשנו בחן ובחסד והחיינו

asher kidshanu b'chen u'va'chesed v'hechi-anu . . .

"who sanctifies us through grace [meaning: providential love]
and unconditional covenantal love, and enlivens / animates / inspirits
us (to). . . ."

This is the God who loves us, and who inspires us, and motivates us, and empowers us in greatest and fullest love. This is **Anochi**!

This is a God to whom I can relate, to whom I can speak.

This is a prayer I can say!

This is the way to talk to **Anochi**, who is the Everything of Everything.

This is the way to talk to **Anochi**, who is our God.

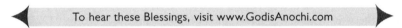

To hear these Blessings, visit www.GodisAnochi.com

When we continually acknowledge **Anochi**, and stay in full gratitude to **Anochi**, we become keenly aware of **Anochi**-energy that permeates our whole world, and **Anochi**-Oneness consciousness that is the guide and goal for ourSelves and for all humanity.

To express the blessings of praise and gratitude we give to **Anochi**, whenever it feels right and good, you can chant: *B'rachot v'ho'da-ot me-atah v'ad olam,* "Blessings and Gratitude to You, **Anochi**. Now and Forever."

To hear this B'rachot, visit www.GodisAnochi.com

Whenever you give **Anochi** praise and thanks, you can ask **Anochi** to hear and accept your words of prayer by chanting, *Sho'me-ah tefilah,* "O, **Anochi**, please listen to my prayer."

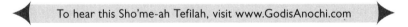

To hear this Sho'me-ah Tefilah, visit www.GodisAnochi.com

In whatever way and whenever you connect with **Anochi**, be with **Anochi** in the fullness of your being.

Then, listen.

Listen well.

Anochi will respond.

Anochi *always* responds.

Because **Anochi** loves you.

KEEPING FAITH WITH **ANOCHI**

Being in Never-ending **Anochi**-Belief

Even with all that there is to be said, experienced, and felt about **Anochi**, doubters, and skeptics, and nonbelievers will remain. Some rationalists and intellectuals will continue to insist on only empirical and existential proofs.

'Twas always thus.

The pendulum of thinking and feeling over the existence, properties, characteristics, and behaviors of God—and humankind's relationship with the Divine—has always swung between belief and nonbelief, surety and uncertainty; between coming to God through faith, and coming to God through reason.

In this age of reason—that is, at the same time, an age of ever-growing faith—you are invited to be open to being a rational intellect with the soul of a mystic.

At this time of high science and technology, when so much genius and power is in human hands, when machines (made, we sometimes tend to forget, by human minds and hands) seem to hold powers even greater than humankind, it is often easy to think that **Anochi** has become irrelevant—that humankind is greater than God.

The Bible anticipates this very scenario when it teaches, "...[do not] say to yourselves, 'My own power and the might of my own hand have won this wealth for me.' Remember that it is the Lord God who gives you the power to get wealth . . ." (Deuteronomy 8:17–18).

It works like this: In the beginning **Anochi** created everything that ever was to be in this world.

Picture a ladder. Everthing that ever was, is, and will be, is on one of the rungs of the ladder. The first human beings—let's call them Adam and Eve—stood at the bottom of the ladder, reached as high as they could, and took what they could from the entirety of creation. Their children stood on their shoulders—and, except for shattered hopes and dreams now and then—were able to reach to higher and higher rungs of the ladder.

And, so it has been for every generation. We stand on the shoulders of the achievements and accomplishments of those who come before us—we don't have to "reinvent the wheel" in every generation—and we reach as high as we can to pluck out what has always been there, and that we are just finding

Think, for a moment, about humankind's progression. Language. Fire. Agriculture. The wheel. Writing. The Earth is round, not flat. The Earth revolves around the sun. Machinery. Germs. Relativity. High technology. All is there, in full truth, from the moment of creation—waiting, just waiting to be discovered. The old "truth" is discarded; the new truth is declared—until a newer truth comes to light, and the climb continues.

That is why today's technological achievement is on the ash heap tomorrow; that is why today's medical breakthrough is outdated tomorrow.

We are creative, but we never create anything *ex nihilo*—from nothing—for that is **Anochi's** role, alone. Rather, we discover that what **Anochi** already put out there has been waiting for us all this time. That is how progress takes place, how the world moves forward. When—in continuing co-creative partnership with **Anochi**—we reach the top of the ladder, we will establish a perfect world: the messianic age will dawn, and Earth will be Eden once again.

Further, from where does every idea, every vision, every "Aha" moment that leads to our creativity, our innovations, our inventions, come? They come from **Anochi**. Some would argue that they come from the greatness of the human brain to think, to process, to imagine, to dream, to feel, but from where does the human brain—with all its capacity and capabilities—come? From **Anochi**.

And, so, the story of the scientists who came to **Anochi** and said,

*"**Anochi**, we are sorry to tell you this. We don't need You anymore. We have found the way to create human beings all by ourselves. Sadly, You have become irrelevant to us."*

Anochi *replied, "Is that so? Please show Me."*

So, one scientist bent down and picked up a clump of rich soil from the ground, and began to shape it and forge it into a human being.

   Anochi *watched for a moment, and then said, "No, no, no. Use your own dirt."*

Dr. Robert Jastrow, the late physicist, astronomer, and head of NASA, America's space program, put it more elegantly—and profoundly: "The scientist has lived by the power of reason. He has scaled the mountains of ignorance, and is about to conquer the highest peak. As he pulls himself over the final rock, he is greeted by a band of theologians who have been sitting there for centuries."

The prophet of old put it decisively: "Not by might, nor by power, but by My Spirit, says the Lord" (Zechariah 2:6).

In this rational world, it is easy to deny the very existence of **Anochi**. In our arrogance or hubris, it is easy to disavow **Anochi**. In our bewilderment over the evils that beset this world, it is easy to repudiate **Anochi**. In our anguish over our own pain and suffering, it is easy to reject **Anochi**.

It is easy to forsake belief. It is easy to lose faith.

Long ago, **Anochi** anticipated that our human power and our creature comforts would lead us away from faith. This was true in days of old and is equally true now.

Moses, speaking in the name of YHWH, who was then **Anochi's** representative on Earth, says,

> When I have brought them into the land . . . flowing with milk and honey, and they have eaten their fill, and waxen fat, and turned to other gods and served them, and despised Me and broken My covenant . . .   —DEUTERONOMY 31:20

> I will hide My face from them, and see what their end will be. For they are a very forward generation, children in whom there is no faithfulness.   —DEUTERONOMY 32:20

When we lack faith, when we turn our faces away from **Anochi**, when we no longer seek to know **Anochi** from the Insides of the Insides, then **Anochi** seems hidden from us; **Anochi** seems lost to us.

But **Anochi** is always there, waiting for us to turn and re-turn in faith.

Some contemporary thinkers and theologians help those who choose to disbelieve by claiming that rational intellect always outweighs blind faith, and that matters of the mind always outweigh imaginings of spirit; that the idea of God is nothing more than the need—and the "creation"— of the human mind; that God is all good, but not all powerful; that God was the "Prime Mover," setting the world in motion, but does not intercede in our lives; that God could not possibly care about every human being, and, thus, cannot possibly be a personal God to each human being; that God is manifest only in nature; that God is reflected only in human relationships; that God is nothing more than the internal energy that inspires human beings to be and do good.

The theological criticisms of these thinkers are not without merit, because they are describing the only God they know—YHWH. And, YHWH *is* limited, for YHWH is only one aspect of the whole God— one panel of the Divine Beach Ball, of **Anochi, I-Source**; only a deputy of **Anochi** here on Earth. When philosophers and theologians and all human beings come to know **Anochi**, they will meet the full Source, and recognize that **Anochi** is the everything of the everything, the entirety of the universe: life and death and life eternal, male and female, sorrow and joy, tragedy and triumph, good and evil, anguish and celebration, engagement and distance, dusk and dawn.

So, we need not be swayed by temporal arguments against God. We need not be moved by age-old contentions that seem to be offered in every generation, yet have always failed to prevail. We need not adopt any of the so-called convenient denials of God. For they are all rendered moot in the recognition that **Anochi** is the whole God.

Anochi, I-Source *is the Whole God.*
Anochi, I *is the Whole* **God Within.**

All that we seek—or refute—is in **Anochi, I-Source.**
All that we seek—or refute—is in **Anochi, I—Anochi Within.**
Our own lives are both witness and testimony.

At our core, we know—*we are*—the refutation to every argument that ignores or rejects **Anochi**; we are the wholeness that embraces the wholeness of **Anochi**; we have the faith that accepts every aspect, every attribute—no matter how troubling or how enhancing—of **Anochi**.

Your own inner journey takes you toward the place where the fullness of **Anochi** resides—the place of sacred space and holy moments. Your own inner journey affirms your faith.

So,

Have faith.

Keep the faith.

Be faith.

To remember and affirm your faith, you can chant, *Ani ma'amin b'emunah sh'leimah* ***B'Anochi.*** "I believe, with perfect faith, in **Anochi**."

◀ To hear this I Believe chant, visit www.GodisAnochi.com ▶

THE FACE IN THE MIRROR IS YOUR OWN

——◁○▷——

A long, long time ago (or maybe it was just yesterday) a very, very poor man—let's call him Joseph, the son of Jacob—who lived in a little village—let's call it WoodLand—had a dream.

In his dream, he was told to go to a big, faraway city—let's call it KingsTown—where he was to look for a treasure that is buried under the bridge that leads to the king's palace.

After dreaming the same dream night after night, he set out for KingsTown to uncover his treasure.

When he arrived in KingsTown, he saw that the bridge was guarded day and night. He could not start digging—or even looking—for his treasure, lest he be caught by the guards. Even so, he kept going to the bridge every morning, and kept walking around it until late every night.

Finally, the captain of the guards asked him—in a very kindly way—if he were looking for something or waiting for someone.

Joseph told him his story—that he had come to KingsTown, bidden by his dream, to search for his treasure under the king's bridge.

The captain laughed and said, "Ah, poor fellow. To please a dream, you wore out your shoes to come here.

"As for having faith in dreams, if I had it, I would follow my dream— the dream I dream night after night. I would go to a little village, far from here, called WoodLand, and dig for my treasure under the house of a fellow named Joseph, son of Jacob.

"But, I can just imagine how difficult that would be. I would have to try every house, for I am sure that half of the folks over there must be named Joseph, and the other half must be named Jacob."

Joseph said farewell to the captain, journeyed back to his village, and dug under his house.

And there, right under his own house, Joseph uncovered his treasure.

—◀○▶—

The Sage teaches:

"What lies behind us, and what lies before us are tiny matters, compared to what lies within us."[1]

PART TWO

DEVELOPING A PERSONAL RELATIONSHIP WITH ANOCHI

SEVEN

ANOCHI WITHIN

Through sacred scholarship, we have explored the Bible, and we have found God's real Name—**Anochi.**

Now, we enter into the world of sacred spirit, to know God—and especially **God Within**—in deep, personal, intimate, loving relationship.

> It is **Anochi's** Breath within you that animates you and gives you life.
> It is **Anochi's** design and plan within you that gives you purpose and direction.
> It is **Anochi's** quiet Voice within you that gives you intention and resolve.
> It is **Anochi's** eternity within you that gives you immortality.

The Hebrew word *kavannah* means "intention." It is used to set a context for studying a sacred text or commentary, for focusing on a meaning or an interpretation of a prayer, teaching, or a holy insight.

Most of all, *kavannah* is your own spiritual intention to center your attention on being in relationship with **Anochi**: to see the wonders of the transcendent, supernatural **Anochi**, through the eyes of the immanent **Anochi Within**; to open yourSelf to the depths of your inner being—your **GodSelf**—in order to touch, experience, feel, be in love with the Ultimate, Eternal Being.

Knowing **Anochi, I-Source** and knowing **Anochi-I, Anochi Within** enflames the sparks of the Divine in the universe and within each of us, and opens us to the infinite possibilities of life and living.

When we act from **Anochi-I**, we are, in the image of the contemporary mystic, "God-ing."[1]

When we are confronted by the tough choices of existence, when we are faced with the decisions—big and small—that make us or break us as human beings, we can view the world and make our choices from the "God-ness" at the core of our beings, the **Anochi-I, God Within**, our GodSelves.

You come into your **GodSelf** when the channel between your small self and **Anochi**, the supernatural, transcendent God, is completely open, so that **Anochi** inundates your self with God. That is why we call it the **GodSelf**.

Your **GodSelf** is your **God-ness**—the deepest, highest, and finest of your God-like being.

In reality, there are no small decisions. Each instant brings us to the big and ever-repeating decision: Will we come to each moment, each encounter, from love? Will we choose to be in judgment or compassion? Will we reject or embrace? Will we opt for separation or Oneness?

Each and every choice determines how our lives, our existence, our whole universe will be, for from our **Anochi-I** GodSelf we are co-creating with **Anochi I-Source** everthing in our world.

> Find, nourish, and celebrate your GodSelf,
>   your **Anochi Within**.
> Find deepest meaning in your life, and greatest joy
>   in your existence.

KNOWING **ANOCHI**

Coming Face to Face with *Anochi's* "I Am" Presence

The age-old question: What is the meaning of life?
Who am I?
What is my reason for being?
What is the meaning of my existence?
What is my role, my purpose, my mission on this Earth?

With all the wise attempts throughout the millennia to respond to this question, there is really only one answer. It is as simple as it is profound.

The meaning of life is to know God.
The reason for being is to know the supernatural, transcendent **Anochi**, and to know the immanent **Anochi Within**.
Meaning in life comes from being in deep, personal, intimate relationship with **Anochi**.
Life's purpose is to live in **Anochi**-energy, and to nurture **Anochi**-consciousness of Oneness.

Now knowing that **Anochi** is the name of God means coming to know the supernatural, transcendent God: the God who creates, commands, and sustains; the God of history and destiny.

And knowing **Anochi** means coming to know the immanent God—the **God Within**.

Knowing that **Anochi** is the Source of All—and at the very same time that **Anochi** is deep within us—means that we and **Anochi** can meet at the "Point of Essence"—the place of ultimate union of the human and the Divine.

It is at the Point of Essence that we and **Anochi** are, in the words of the poet, "like two waves rolling over each other and interwetting each other."[2]

It is here where the singular Oneness of each soul crosses the abyss and knows that there is no distance to the Infinite Oneness of **Anochi**. Here, we come into union, into Being, with **Anochi**; we merge with universal, eternal knowledge; we intuitively feel and sense the innermost secrets of the universe. We are bathed in **Anochi's** Light, and then we become mirror-reflections of the Light of the Divine.

Like Cain, we engage **Anochi-I** to affirm our place in the universe, and to affirm our responsibility to other human beings.

Like Abraham, Isaac, Jacob, and Moses, we engage **Anochi-I** to be our internal compass, directing, guiding, and protecting our journeys.

Like Abraham and his servant, we engage **Anochi-I** to find love, and like Isaac and Rebecca, we engage **Anochi-I** to live love.

Like Sarah, Rebecca, and Rachel, we engage **Anochi-I** to become pregnant with the infinite possibilities of creation.

Like Esau, we engage **Anochi-I** to satisfy our spiritual hunger.

Like Jacob, we engage **Anochi-I** to demonstrate our true sincerity.

Like Joseph, we engage **Anochi-I** to get in touch with our feelings of acceptance and compassion.

Like Moses, we engage **Anochi-I** to rise up to the task at hand, and to face any burden or trial.

Like Pharaoh, we engage **Anochi-I** to overcome our stubbornness, and to soften our hardened hearts.

Like Balaam, we engage **Anochi-I** to find blessing in life.

> So I looked for You in the holy place . . .
> My soul thirsts for You. (Psalms 63:2–3)

At the holy Bush, **Anochi** identifies **AnochiSelf** as infinity—"I Am That I Am" (Exodus 3:14). "I Was; I Am Now; I Always Will Be. In Me is the wholeness, the totality, the Oneness of Everything That Is."

"I Am."

Anochi is the "I Am" Presence.

Not directly in the Torah-text, but implied in the story is that
Anochi then asks Moses, "Who are you?"

And, Moses replies, "I Am That I Am."

Moses knows the full Essence of **Anochi** within himself; he is the
mirror-reflection of the Light of the Divine.

Anochi sees this, and knows that Moses is the right man for the
job!

As with Moses, in each one of us is the "I Am" Presence.

The "I Am" Presence is **Anochi-I, Anochi Within.**

Here is a simple yet profound prayer we can recite to begin to awaken
and touch the **Anochi-I, Anochi Within.** Its language reminds us of
the inextricably intertwined, interweaving of God and **God Within.**

Each day—every day—you can say this prayer, "Rejoicing in **Anochi
Within.**"

*I lift my eyes
to the Light in my soul.*

*I center my love
in the Heart of my heart.*

*I bind my spirit
to the Presence Within.*

*Breath of all Breath,
Life of all Life,*

*I Am of You.
The one of the One.*

*You are in me.
The One of the one.*

*And One Voice sings:
"I Am That I Am."*

WD

To remember the "I Am" place where **Anochi-I** and **Anochi, I-Source** meet, you can chant, "I Am. I Am. I Am That I Am."

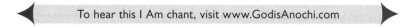

To hear this I Am chant, visit www.GodisAnochi.com

BEING ONE WITH **ANOCHI**

Connecting with the Breath of **Anochi**

The religious and cultural mind-set that many of us inherited—based in great part from the biblical behavior of YHWH-*Adonai*—is that God is "Up There." God is the supernatural, transcendent God of the Heavens, separate and distinct from human beings—who chooses when and how to descend into life on this Earth.

Now that we know that **Anochi, I-Source** is the whole God, and being fully aware that **Anochi-I** is the **God Within**, our sense of God is not only challenged, but can be puzzling.

If God is everything, and since I, the elephant, and the chair are part of everything, then I, the elephant, and the chair are God. Right?

Some—especially in this the new age—would say, "That is exactly right. You are God."

I would say, "Not quite." We do not claim an undifferentiated Oneness with God. Yes, God is everywhere. God is *in* the elephant. The elephant is *of* God. God is *in* the chair. The chair is *of* God. God is *in* me. I am *of* God. My breath is the Breath of God. My spirit is the Spirit of God. God is within me, but I am not God. I am not **Anochi**.

To remind yourself that it is **Anochi**—and **Anochi** alone—who is the Creator and Redeemer of every living soul, you can sing, *Bo-rei v'Go-el kol haNeshamot,* "Creator and Redeemer of each and every Soul."

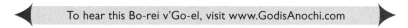

To hear this Bo-rei v'Go-el, visit www.GodisAnochi.com

We want to know **Anochi** and be with **Anochi** from "the Inside of the Insides." We want **Anochi** to be at the very center of our beings.

And **Anochi** needs and wants all of us to be part of the Divine, to be wholly of **Anochi**. **Anochi** wants us to be in the "Inside of the

Insides," to reside at the Heart of all Being, to be Within **Anochi**, to be at the very center of **Anochi's** Being.

So, in finding and connecting with **Anochi Within**, we seek the most intimate union with **Anochi**.

We seek to merge ourSelves with **Anochi's** Self, our being with **Anochi's** Being. We want to come into alignment, attunement, at-One-ment, with **Anochi**. We want to be in the deepest spiritual intention, the highest spiritual connection, the highest and the deepest human consciousness. We want to be wholly present in **Anochi's** design and flow, in **Anochi's** energy field, **Anochi's** light-sphere, **Anochi's** wave-length. We want to be a conduit to **Anochi** and a channel of **Anochi**.

How do we come into this kind of intimacy with **Anochi**? How do we touch and embrace **Anochi Within**?

At the moment of Creation, *Ruach*, "the breath, the spirit, of God" hovered over the waters. At the moment of the creation of *Adam Kadmon*, the very first human being, God "blew into his nostrils the soul/breath of life, and he became a living soul" (Genesis 1:2 and 2:7).

The breath of **Anochi** is the life force of human beings. We exist, we live, because our breath is the breath of **Anochi**. "You send forth Your Breath, O God, and we are created. You take away our breath and we die and return to the dust" (after Ecclesiastes 12:7).

Like the biblical Joseph, we are all people "in whom the spirit—the breath—of God dwells" (Genesis 41:38).

When we are mindful of our breathing, when we pay close attention to each breath, when we listen carefully and hear our breath within us, we can become very aware of **Anochi Within**.

The very Hebrew word for breath, *ruach*—pronounced *roo-ach* (the *ach* is a guttural as in Johann Sebastian B*ach*)—sounds the whoosh of air, the InBreath and OutBreath of natural breathing.

When we breathe with full cognizance and intention, we can merge our breath with **Anochi's** breath. That puts us in closest connection with **Anochi**, and attunes ourSelves to **Anochi's** harmonic ebb and flow for the universe.

And there is more. Not only are we in touch with **Anochi-I**,

Within, but we are the complete partners with **Anochi** in breathing in the conscious existence—the entire Being—of creation.

Here is how this works: **Anochi** breathes **Anochi's** Breath; you breathe your breath. But, the breaths are not individual; they are not separate. You and **Anochi** share one breath; you breathe the same breath together. **Anochi's** OutBreath is your InBreath. Your OutBreath is **Anochi's** InBreath.

Can you imagine anything more intimate, anything more ardent?

And what does this in-sync breathing do? It breathes the essence of **Anochi-ness** into every cell of your being, and into every space and place in creation.

You are fully aware: As at the very moment of the creation of the world, at the moment of your creation as a human being on this Earth, and at every moment of your existence, you are One with **Anochi**.

There is a simple chant—the word *Ruach* (meaning "breath/spirit") and the word "Breathing"—which can help you be in touch with your breath, with the Breath of **Anochi, I-Source**, and with **Anochi-I, Anochi Within**.

◄ To hear Ruach/Breathing, visit www.GodisAnochi.com ►

JOURNEYING TO **ANOCHI** WITHIN

Spiraling to **Anochi** through the Tree of Life

In our book *20-Minute Kabbalah: The Daily Personal Spiritual Practice That Brings You To God, Your Soul-Knowing, and Your Heart's Desires*, my wife and coauthor, Ellen Kaufman Dosick, and I offer a new model for the ancient Kabbalistic Tree of Life.

Kabbalah is one of Judaism's most powerful mystical traditions. It is an incredibly elaborate, deep, and complex spiritually based theological system that has been hidden away for centuries, and is just now re-emerging in this modern age of spiritual renaissance and renewal. At its core is a unique worldview that explains the relationship between God, the universe, and humankind.

The Tree of Life is the Kabbalah's pathway for God in the high Heavens and human beings here on Earth to connect. The traditional Tree of Life—often illustrated imposed on human form—is linear and hierarchical. Through a series of *sefirot*—steps, or emanations—God "comes down" to meet humankind, while humankind "goes up" to meet God.

In this emerging egalitarian age, this time of weaving of webs and intertwining networks, this linear model does not speak to us. So, we have re-envisioned the Tree of Life to be a spiral. Beginning in the center—in *Tiferet,* the Heart Space *sefirah*—the journey to and from God weaves through the human body and the universe in a continually moving, swirling, spinning, interweaving, vibrating spiral.

> Take the inner journey through the Spiral Tree of Life.
> Feel the spiral move through your body.
> At each of these places in your body is a *sefirah,* a gateway, a
>   connection with the Divine.
> Begin in your heart;
> now move to the left of your heart;
> and now circle across your body to the right of your heart.
> Now, let the spiral continue down to your right hip;
> and now circle across your body to your left hip.
> Now, let the spiral continue up to your left shoulder;
> and now circle across your body to your right shoulder.
> From there, let the spiral continue all the way down to your
>   second chakra, just below your belly button.
> Now, the spiral shifts from a horizontal plane to a plane of
>   depth—no longer moving between left and right, but
>   between front and back.
> So now, spiral from your second chakra up your back, to the
>   back of your High Heart (just above your heart).
> Now, continue the spiral through your High Heart, out your
>   front, and down to your Omega chakra, at your ankles.
> Now, zoom the spiral from your ankles all the way up to your
>   Crown chakra, at the top of your head.

And, finally, spiral past your face, into the front of your High
    Heart (just above your heart).
Can you feel the circling, the spiraling, the constant move-
    ment, the unending progression?
Can you feel your body's rotation merging with the rotation
    of the Earth, its swaying with the rhythms of creation, its
    encircling of the never-ending circle?
Can you feel the connection, the interweaving, of your
    body—and your soul—with God?
The Spiral Tree of Life carries you in Divine design, in Divine
    flow, on the inner journey to **Anochi Within**.

The spiral is like the Kabbalah's Name for God—*Ein Sof.* It is Infinite—
without beginning and without end; always and forever.

And, we know the name *Ein Sof* was the mystics' best understanding of the concept of **Anochi**—the whole, complete, Eternal God; the
full Essence of the God of Everything.

So, the journey to **Anochi Within** is not the outward journey up
the traditional Tree of Life to the transcendent God (as important and
vital as is that journey). Rather, it is an inner journey, spiraling through
the multidimensional Spiral Tree of Life that is your being, your nature,
your reflection of the delicate, elegant dance of life.

There you will find whatever you always knew, but which you—
through the vicissitudes of everyday life on Earth—may have forgotten. **Anochi Within**, the God within you—you!—is of boundless
space and time, dazzling beauty, and unlimited potentiality. In you
is the entire universe, unfolding in perfect order—because God is
within you.

There are many ways to journey within. In *20-Minute Kabbalah,* we
offer one kind of daily practice (chant, meditation, and prayer) that
many have found very helpful. There are myriad other pathways. You
may well find and develop your own.

Whatever kind of practice or pathway ultimately works for you, it is—not to be too trite—not the destination, but the journey that is important. God *is* within you, waiting to be found, waiting to be embraced, waiting to be partnered.

Without each other, both **Anochi** and you will be lonely. With each other, you will be in the deepest, most intimate, most precious, relationship of your life on this Earth.

The journey on the mystical inner pathway is a journey that deserves and is worthy of every bit of your energy. For, when you find the psychic connection to **Anochi Within**, you go, in the poetic-image of our great Rebbe Shlomo Carlebach *zt"l,* "beyond the beyond, to the highest of the high, and the deepest of the deep."

To bring yourSelf to **Anochi**-awareness as much and as often as possible, you can chant *"Bakshu **Anochi** Tamid"*—"Seek **Anochi's** Face (Being/Presence) All-Ways" (adaptation of Psalms 105:4, lit: "Seek His Face All-Ways").

> ◀ To hear this Bakshu chant, visit www.GodisAnochi.com ▶

BEING IN **ANOCHI'S** PURPOSE AND PLAN

Embracing **Anochi's** Design

Ours is a freewill universe, but it is not a random universe. There are no accidents, no coincidences.

Anochi created us and our world with purpose and plan.

> Before I created you in the womb, I selected you; Before you were
> born, I consecrated you.   —JEREMIAH 1:5

Yet, the limitations of mind and body on Earth, and the space-time boundaries of human existence, make it almost impossible for us to see the blueprint and design.

The late rabbi and writer Chaim Potok *zt"l* explains it this way (in an era before egalitarian language): "The seeing of God is not like the seeing of man. Man sees only between the blinks of his eyes. He does not know what the world is like between the blinks. He sees the world in pieces, in fragments. But, God sees the world whole, unbroken . . . Our seeing is broken. Can we make it like the world of God?"[3]

The late mystic Rabbi Abraham Joshua Heschel *zt"l* answers (in the same nonegalitarian language of his day) by suggesting that every once in a while, we are given glimpses of God's eternal plan. "God is not always silent, and man is not always blind. In every man's life, there are moments when there is a lifting of the veil of the horizon of the unknown, opening a sight of the eternal."[4]

When we pray, and meditate, and chant, and dance, and learn, and celebrate, when we immerse in the beauty and grandeur of mountain and sea, and field and forest, and the stark isolation of the desert, it is then that we travel channels into **Anochi's** Holy Presence; it is then we can open ourSelves to those glimpses—to those moments in between the blinks—where we can see fragments and slivers of the Divine design.

The sages of the Talmud (Babylonian Talmud, *Sanhedrin* 106b), whose seeing was finely honed, guided us toward the way of grasping **Anochi's** plan: "God desires the heart."

Anochi, I-Source is the Heart of Hearts, the reality that all is Love; Love is all. It is **Anochi, I-Source's** purpose and plan that our world be built in the Heart and be sustained by Love.

God desires a *"lev tahor"*—"a pure heart" (Psalms 24:4).

When we are able to go to the deepest places of our **Anochi-I**, our **God Within**, then we recognize that our mission on Earth is to stand in the Heart, to grow a pure Heart; to be Love, and to bring Love.

How do we best bring ourSelves to the Heart? How do we best fashion a "pure heart"? How do we best manifest **Anochi's** purpose and plan for us and our world?

We learn from the sages (Babylonian Talmud, *Berachot* 7a) who ask, "What does God pray to GodSelf?" They answer, "God says, 'May it be My will that My sense of compassion outweigh My sense of strict justice.'" A modern spiritual guide teaches that we can adapt that prayer for ourselves and say, "May my higher Self (Divine soul) overcome my lower Self (ego) so that I can have compassion for all people."[5]

So, we go to those deepest places of **Anochi Within**, and touch the unconditional love and abiding compassion that live there.

Then, we imitate **Anochi's** Love.

In Love, **Anochi** created and continually re-creates us and our universe.

> In Love, our **Anochi Within** can share in the sacred task of co-creating the generations, and guide us to create lives of meaning and worth.

In Love, **Anochi** sustains the cosmos.

> In Love, our **Anochi Within** can nurture the visions and the values that build up, preserve, and renew our world.

In Love, **Anochi** gives us directives to shape and ennoble our existence.

> In Love, our **Anochi Within** can bring us to the highest energies in ourSelves, inspiring us to be good and to do right.

In Love, **Anochi** promises to redeem the world, and to bring salvation.

> In Love, our **Anochi Within** can impel us to repair and heal the brokenness that plagues our planet and people, and build anew, a perfect world of harmony and Oneness.

It is told (Isaiah 6:3) that the *Seraphim,* the great angels, stand on either side of the Heavenly Throne and call out to each other across the universe their overflowing love for **Anochi:** *"Kadosh, Kadosh, Kadosh,"* *"Sanctus, Sanctus, Sanctus,"* "Holy, Holy, Holy." By chanting the awesome holiness of **Anochi**, they create the Love Vibration, and then they send the Love Vibration from the Heavens to Earth.

We can imitate the *Seraphim*—we can become Earthly angels—by chanting, *Kadosh, Kadosh, Kadosh*—"Holy, holy, holy." In doing so our intent and the timbre of our voices become the channel on which the Love Vibration flows from Heaven to Earth, and anchors **Anochi's** Love in our world.

Our own **Anochi Within** is suffused with Love; we are Love.

It is said that every *Seraph* has at least thirty-six sets of wings:

Feel the power and the glory of your own angel wings, stand with the *Seraphim,* stand with **Anochi,** and chant *Kadosh.*

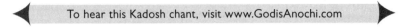

To hear this Kadosh chant, visit www.GodisAnochi.com

Yet, even the purest heart, even the finest love, can sometimes be led astray. So, our oft-recited prayer is "Purify my heart to serve You *in truth.*"

Anochi's truth is eternal—not subject to the vagaries of time or place; not dependent on shifting ideas, opinions, fads, or political correctness of the moment.

So, we seek the truth of our **Anochi Within**—not the limited view of our human experience, but the entirety of **Anochi**-perspective; not the temporal boundaries of finite existence, but the greatness and grandeur of infinite and eternal reality.

Our search for ultimate truth—which we demand of ourselves—is what takes us from ordinary, everyday interaction influenced by relativity and shaped by our human needs, desires, and emotions, and calls us to the depths of our **Anochi Within**, where infinite and eternal truth reside.

The foundation of existence is **Anochi's** ultimate truth. The foundation of our existence is living truth.

And so, we seek to serve **Anochi** truly, in the truest way we know; in the way that is in accordance with Divine design.

And, just as knowledge is ever-unfolding, truth is ever-emerging. Truth flows through the Time Tunnel of enlightenment, where tiny pieces of the secrets of the universe are revealed, and smidgens of the mysteries of existence are grasped. Your **Anochi Within** is enlarged and extended. You see ancient truth filtered through new prisms. New truths emerge that add new wisdom to the collective consciousness, and become part of All That Is. You are a living gateway between Heaven and Earth.

So, all we need do is embrace what the modern prayer asks and answers, and what our **Anochi Within** surely knows: "Who are we? We are Light, and Truth, and Infinite Wisdom, Eternal Goodness."[6]

When we stay in **Anochi's** design, when we stay fully connected to

Anochi, I-Source and energize **Anochi Within**, we are aligned with **Anochi's** blueprint for us and our world.

Anything else that we might do—any movement away from **Anochi's** design—is a breach of **Anochi's** purpose and plan, and puts us out of integrity with **Anochi Within**. Our inner compass wavers, and our souls are bruised. When we fall out of alignment with the Divine flow, we experience existential angst and loneliness, and risk violating **Anochi's** eternal intent.

Sometimes we rebuff **Anochi's** will; sometimes we try to hide from it; sometimes we try to overturn it.

An old story—updated for contemporary times:

> A man was walking in a shopping mall in Los Angeles when he saw the Angel of Death standing in front of him. The Angel raised up his massive wings as if to embrace and take the man, so the man turned and ran for his life.
>
> He came home and told his children what had happened, and then announced that he was immediately making a plane reservation to fly to Chicago to avoid the Angel of Death.
>
> After he left for the airport, his children went to the mall to find the Angel of Death and inquire as to why their father was to die.
>
> When they found the Angel of Death, they asked, "Why did you raise your wings to take our father? He is such a good man; he doesn't deserve to die, especially here in this sterile, impersonal shopping mall."
>
> And the Angel of Death replied, "I did not raise my wings to take your father. It was just that I was so surprised to see him here. You see, I have an appointment with him tonight in Chicago."

Sometimes, we pervert **Anochi's** perfect plan and wound our **Anochi Within**.

We forget that "**Anochi's** will is **Anochi's** will." Our egos, our pretenses, our shadows, our fears, get in the way, and we try to convince **Anochi** that our will—the things we want and desire—should be **Anochi's** will.

Sadly, in our contemporary world, we see examples of this all too often, as individuals and groups declare that their will is God's will. When they try to foist their will on others, it leads to fundamentalism, which leads to extremism, which leads to terrorism. And our world is in fear, and cries out in pain.

Yet, our **Anochi Within** knows that it is **Anochi** who decides what is right and wrong, what is in the highest and best interest of us and our world—including that which is in each person's highest good. And, at the same time, we accept that our human emotions—which are subject to the capriciousness of life—will fully experience the delicate balance between pain and joy, tragedy and triumph.

So, as President Abraham Lincoln once put it, "I want to humbly pray that we are on God's side."[7]

And, as Rabbi Heschel *zt"l* taught, "Prayer is not man imposing his will on God. It is God imposing His will—and mercy—on man."[8]

Put most succinctly, "Thy will be done."[9]

How do we best co-create **Anochi's** purpose and plan for this world?

We step into the Void.

What is the Void? It sounds like a scary place, empty and full of uncertainty and chaos. Why should we go there?

Actually, the Void is the awesome and magnificent place of creation.

Only in that dark, hidden place—the womb of a mother, the underground of a planted seed—can creation begin and growth come. The Void is filled with potentiality.

When we go into **Anochi's** Void, to the "Inside of the Inside," we come into co-creation with **Anochi**. We align our beings with Divine design, and dance with God in the ever-continuing act of creation.

*We are like the woman who dreamed that she walked into a new shop in the marketplace, and, to her great surprise, she found **Anochi** behind the counter.*

"What do You sell here?" she asked.

*"Everything your heart desires," replied **Anochi**.*

"That is just wonderful," said the woman. "If that is so, then I want peace of mind, and love, and wisdom, and happiness, and freedom from fear."

After a moment, she added, "Not just for me. For everyone on Earth."

***Anochi** smiled. "I think you have Me wrong, my dear. We don't sell fruits here. Only seeds."*

Our **Anochi-I, Anochi Within** is **Anochi's** Earthly gardener. And, with loving determination, we say to **Anochi, I-Source**, "May our seeds be like You."

To best remember and imprint on your being your place in **Anochi's** purpose and plan, you can say this prayer for "Being in Divine Design." Speak to **Anochi, I-Source**, and speak to **Anochi Within**.

Anochi, Anochi,
Here I Am,
but flesh and blood,
yet You formed me in Your Image.
Here I Am,
but dust and ashes,
yet You have made me just a little lower than the angels.

Still,
In the vastness of the universe,
and in the thick of the human arena,
I am often uncertain and afraid.
I feel my frailty.

So,
*Please, **Anochi**, please:*
When fear grips me,
and anxiety holds me tight,

show me the way to my heart.
Show me the way to the Heart of Hearts.
Show me the way to faith and trust.

When I walk in the valley of the shadows,
and sadness threatens to overwhelm me,
show me the way to the light.
Show me the way to the Light of Lights.
Show me the way to hope and joy.

For,
even with my limitations and my disquiet,
and in the tumult of the human drama,
I am also aware of my boundless potential.
I sense my greatness.

So,
When I use my proficiency and my power
to enhance and ennoble
Your Eternal Plan,
enable me, empower me, and strengthen me.

And,
When my pride, or vanity, or arrogance
subvert Your will or imperil Your design,
show me the way to my soul.
Show me the way to the Soul of Souls.
Show me the way to discernment and truth.

This day and every day,
Anochi,
give me
the wisdom, humility, and courage
to avow and say:

"Thy will be done."
"Thy will be done."
"Thy will be done."

And, always, always
show me the way to love.
Show me the way to the Love of Love.
For Love is All; All is Love.
Love is All; All is Love.
Amen.

WD

Whether you are in the valley of the shadows, or if you are at the pinnacle of the heights, you can be in **Anochi's** flow, and embrace **Anochi's** design. You can dwell with **Anochi**; you can live in **Anochi's** House.

To remember where you live, you can chant, *"V'shavti b'veit Anochi."* "I place myself in **Anochi's** care" (adaptation of Psalms 23:6).

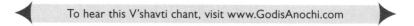

To hear this V'shavti chant, visit www.GodisAnochi.com

ANOCHI CARES

Feeling **Anochi's** Love

When we know the real name of God, when we know **Anochi**, then we know a God who cares deeply about each and every human being.

We can resonate with a God who, in Torah, gives us an ethical mandate to do what is right: feed the hungry; care for the widow and the orphan; tell truth; give fair weights and measures; pay a day laborer at the end of the day, so that person can have enough to eat. We can respond to a God who tells us to honor our parents; to be kind to the stranger; to not put a stumbling block before the blind; and to love our neighbor as we love ourselves.[10]

Then, we who are created "in the Image of **Anochi**," can imitate **Anochi**.

In the words of the modern writer, Alan Paton, we can pray:

O God,
> open my eyes that I may see the needs of others;
> open my ears that I may hear their cries;
> open my heart so that they may not be without solace.
> Let me not be afraid to defend the weak because of the
> > anger of the strong;
> nor afraid to defend the poor because of the anger of the rich.
> Show me where love, and hope, and faith are needed,
> and use me to bring them to those places.
> And so open my eyes and ears
> that I may, this coming day, be able to do some work of
> > peace for You.[11]

Then, in the words of the modern prayer-writer Rabbi Jules Harlow, based on the ancient teachings of the prophets and sages (and modified to speak **Anochi's** name), our **Anochi-I**, our **God Within**, is called to action—to challenge and greatness.

As **Anochi** is gracious and compassionate,
You be gracious and compassionate.
Help the needy bride, visit the sick;
Comfort the mourners, attend to the dead.
Share your bread with the hungry,
Take the homeless into your home.
Help those who have no help;
Be eyes to the blind, feet to the lame.
What is hateful to you, do not do to your fellow;
But love your neighbor as yourself.
Love peace and pursue peace,
Love your fellow creatures, and draw them close to you.

As **Anochi** is gracious and compassionate,
You be gracious and compassionate.[12]

Our **Anochi Within** is most manifest when we are human and humane, when we extend greatest decency and dignity to every human being.

To remember this mandate to goodness, you can chant, *"Chen Va'Chesed, V'Rachamim"*—"Grace, Love, and Compassion."

> Grace: Providential Love—being open to receiving God's Love and giving Love to all whom you meet
>
> Love: God's unconditional Love for being in holy covenant with the Divine
>
> Compassion: Walking with another in equal step, especially in pain and suffering

◄ To hear Chen Va'Chesed, visit www.GodisAnochi.com ►

SEEING THE WHOLE **ANOCHI**

Accepting **Anochi's** Attributes of Good and Evil

For many, the greatest impediment to belief in—and embrace of—**Anochi** is the existence of evil. How can a loving God permit such unspeakable evil in this world?

Yet, the ancient prophet conveys the reality:

> I Am God. There is nothing else. I form light and create darkness;
> I make peace and create evil. I, the Source and Substance of All,
> do this.   —Isaiah 45:6–7

That is why the biblical Job asked, "Should we accept only good from God and not accept evil?" (Job 2:10).

Knowing that **Anochi** is the wholeness of the universe, we now understand that everything—everything—is part of God—including what we perceive as evil.

Evil is not a sinister outside force; it is one aspect of God—one of the colored panels of the Divine Beach Ball—and, thus, since we are created "in the Image of **Anochi**," evil is a part of us too.

The evil we perceive has many faces.

Some define natural disasters—earthquakes, hurricanes, fires, floods—as evil. After all, they disrupt and devastate our lives.

Yet, they are all part of the natural order of the universe that **Anochi** created, the ebb and flow of our world as it unfolds. So-called natural disasters are really only natural events, except that human beings are in the way. It may be beautiful to live in San Francisco, and it may be productive to live on the banks of the Mississippi River, but it may not be smart. **Anochi** did not tell us to build our cities and homes in areas that are prone to the regular—and often destructive to us—forces of nature.

Our **Anochi**-given free will and our growing **Anochi Within** wisdom reveal to us ways to tame and contain the damages caused by natural events. Our evolving human consciousness gives us ways to fix the broken and anticipate and shore up against the next onslaught; we build skyscrapers on ball bearings, and build dams, flood walls, and levees, and use fireproof building materials. When we intervene, and are able to retard and diminish nature's mighty power, we are on the way to defeating the pain and despair we feel when nature's capriciousness strikes.

Surely, some of the responsibility for what the insurance companies fondly call "acts of God," lies with us. When we forget or ignore our **Anochi Within** and strip the land of her minerals, choke her skies with our smog, pollute the waters with our waste, and bombard the ozone layer with our spray cans, then it should not surprise us when **Anochi's** carefully constructed and balanced environment is threatened with ecological ruin, and our lives are (sometimes literally) turned upside down.

When we soak **Anochi's** pristine lands with the blood of our wars and killings, we should not be surprised when the earth cries out in her pain.

--◄o►--

Some define the randomness of life, illness, and death—the young mother who develops breast cancer, the young father who drops dead on the tennis court—as evil.

Indeed, we feel the almost unbearable pain when the impact of these tragedies sends us to the pits of anguish.

Yet, our **Anochi**-given evolving human consciousness is unlocking the mysteries of existence; the breakthroughs in science, technology, and medicine are giving us healings and cures. The diseases that killed us yesterday are eradicated today; that which kills us today will be vanquished tomorrow. Slowly, but profoundly, we are getting in touch with our **Anochi Within,** and fixing the ills and evils that beset us.

Since the exile of Adam and Eve from the Garden of Eden, **Anochi** has never promised life on Earth without death; not one of us will live here forever. **Anochi** has never promised life without pain and anguish; not one of us will live in uninterrupted bliss.

Anochi *has* promised—and given—us the ability to conquer, and eventually overcome, what we perceive as the random evil that strikes our lives.

In Torah, **Anochi** sets a choice: "Behold, I set before you this day a blessing and a curse" (Deuteronomy 11:26).

What **Anochi** is saying is: "I am showing you all of my necessary but opposing attributes; all the colored panels of My Divine Beach Ball. Here is the panel of good—the panel of blessing. And, here is the panel of evil—the panel of curse. Choose. Which will be dominant in your life? Will you more often imitate My aspect of good or My aspect of evil?"

Far, far too often in the course of human history, men and women—using their God-given free will—have chosen evil over good. Far, far too often, others have suffered greatly for perverse choices.

In the face of evil the real questions are not, "Where is **Anochi**? How could **Anochi** let this happen?" The real questions are, "Where are human beings? How could human beings let this happen? Where is **Anochi Within?**"

The evils that beset us and our world—poverty, hunger, illiteracy, rape, and murder; oppression, tyranny, and genocide—all come from the acts or the indifference of human beings.

Evil done by human beings can be done by error or accident, knowingly or unwittingly. **Anochi** does not fail to tighten the bolts so that the brakes fail; human beings do. **Anochi** does not drive drunk and kill; human beings do. **Anochi** does not ignore the slums, or the starving masses; human beings do. **Anochi** does not start wars; human beings do.

Evil that is done by human beings is sourced in the foibles, flaws, and failings of the human psyche and spirit. People foist evil on others—sometimes, the most horrific and heinous evil—because of (choose one or many): utter ignorance, fear, greed, the need for power, perverse pleasure, self-righteousness, addiction, compulsion, and worst of all, lack of conscience.

When people force their inhumanity on other human beings, **Anochi, I-Source** metaphorically weeps in the Heavens, and **Anochi-I, God Within** is debased in human spirit and diminished in GodSelf.

Again, Laurence Cossé, in *A Corner of the Veil*—with my emendations to make her language both egalitarian and universal:

> God is indifferent to evil?
>
> God accepts everything, since God is the source of everything. But, God suffers everything. There is no difference between the suffering of human beings and the suffering of God. And God risks everything in creation. Because it is totality, creation carries within itself the germs of its own destruction. God is at stake here. The children not only save humankind, but in some way, they also save God. They justify God's creation.[13]

And, most, we need to remember that **Anochi** has a blueprint and vision for this world. Yet, with our limited human capabilities, we can only see a tiny portion of that plan.

Take, for example, the biblical story of Joseph and his brothers. We very well might perceive the actions of the brothers and of the Egyptian accuser as evil, and surely when Joseph was in the pit and the prison, he was not a very happy man. Yet, he understood. His painful experience was actually part of **Anochi's** ultimate plan. Near the end of the tale, he says to his brothers, "Do not be distressed or reproach yourselves because you sold me here, for God has sent me ahead of you in order to preserve life" (Genesis 45:5, 7–9).

Indeed, during the famine that struck Egypt, because Joseph was already there, the entire Jewish tribe—Jacob and his family—was saved from starvation and destruction. And, because they were saved, they were able to remain in Egypt, and grow in numbers. Eventually, they were enslaved, and then they were redeemed; they came to Mt. Sinai to receive **Anochi's** word, and their descendants came into the Promised Land, the Land of Israel. The survival of the fledgling Jewish people, the giving of **Anochi's** law, and the fulfillment of the covenantal promise of the land all depended on Joseph's story unfolding exactly when, where, and how it did—despite Joseph's personal pain, or our perception of evil that befell him. Joseph was right when he said, ". . . you intended to do evil to me, but God meant it for good" (Genesis 50:20).

If we had the luxury, as we have with Joseph's story, to look down on our own life stories from a more than 3,000-year vantage point, then we might very well see how our own pain and anguish—and what we perceive as evil—fit into **Anochi's** ultimate plan, and how our contribution, even with the deep suffering of our human emotions, moves the world forward in its journey toward the fulfillment of **Anochi's** Divine design.

When—and only when—we are deeply in touch with our **Anochi Within**, can we get glimpses of what was, what is, and what will be. We can hear and see and dream what is not of the moment, not for our own temporal satisfaction, but what is for the ultimate good of our world. And we can see our individual place in the greater plan. No matter how much life sometimes hurts, we embrace the reality of our **Anochi-I, God Within**, and know that in the fullness of our being, both good and evil are part of our wholeness. And then, the real test of our being is not the challenges that confront us, but how we respond and overcome those challenges—all for the greater good.

When we realize that evil is part of the wholeness of **Anochi, I-Source**, and thus, part of our **AnochiSelves**, then we can know how we human beings can work with **Anochi**, so that **Anochi**—and we—choose good more often than evil, so that the good aspects of the Divine, and of humans created "in the Image," prevail over the aspect of evil.

Here is a prayer for "Avoiding Evil and Embracing the Good." When you recite it, it can remind you to touch the very best of your **Anochi-I, God Within**, and it can send your energy right out to the universe, against evil, and for decency and goodness.

> *Anochi, Anochi,*
> *With Your good counsel and steadfast guidance,*
> *Direct me aright.*
>
> *Keep me far from wrong and evil;*
> *keep me far from hatred and wickedness;*
> *keep me far from transgression and sin.*
>
> *Bring me near to goodness and righteousness;*
> *bring me near to justice and honor;*
> *bring me near to integrity and virtue.*
>
> *Give me the strength to oppose malicious design,*
> *the vision to champion the noble cause,*
> *and the conviction to persist in my ideals.*
>
> *Help me be ever-truthful and trustworthy*
> *in thought, in word, and in deed.*
> *Give me the courage to resist temptation,*
> *and the fortitude to fulfill my resolve.*
>
> *Help keep me in clear conscience,*
> *so that no disgracing shame plagues my days.*
> *Help keep me free from guile,*
> *so that no fear of detection disturbs my sleep.*

Help me be slow to anger,
swift to praise,
bountiful in compassion,
abundant in kindness.

Bless me with wisdom of mind,
serenity of spirit,
a passionate soul,
and a heart filled with love.

*And, please **Anochi**, please*
Guide me to live my prayer,
so that in the quiet of eternity,
I can face You.

Amen.

WD

Be good. Do good.

To remember to do good and to avoid evil, and to make your life into the fullness of rich blessing, you can chant, *"Darshu tov, v'al ra, l'man tich'yu."* "Seek good and not evil, that you may live" (adaptation of Amos 5:14).

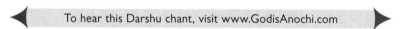

To hear this Darshu chant, visit www.GodisAnochi.com

WRESTLING WITH **ANOCHI**

Affirming Your Place with **Anochi**

Like Jacob of old, we are God-wrestlers.

Our relationship with **Anochi, I-Source** and our relationship with **Anochi-I, God Within**, will ripen, grow, and deepen, and—like any relationship with mutual expectations and responsibilities—there will be times of burden and glory, bitter disappointment and great joy, bewilderment and certainty.

Elie Wiesel—Holocaust survivor, conscience of a generation, prolific author, Nobel Peace Laureate—teaches us that we can be angry with God, disappointed by God, outraged by God. But, never can we ignore God.[14]

The poet Aaron Zeitlin put it this way:

Praise Me, says God, and I will know that you love Me.
Curse Me, says God, and I will know that you love Me.
Praise Me or curse Me,
And I will know that you love Me.

Sing out My graces, says God,
Raise your fist against Me and revile, says God.
Sing out graces or revile,
Reviling is also a kind of praise, says God.

But if you sit fenced off in your apathy, says God,
If you sit entrenched in: "I don't care at all," says God,
If you look at the stars and yawn, says God,
If you see suffering and don't cry out,
If you don't praise and you don't revile,
Then I created you in vain, says God.[15]

So, we will struggle and strive to be with **Anochi.**
There will be times when we must wrestle.
We hope that it will be in dignity, wisdom, gratitude, and humility.
Yet, we know that, sometimes, it will be in anger and anguish.
Either way, wrestle we must.

And you know that much of the time the hardest struggle will be with **Anochi-I, God Within**, for who is harder on you than yourSelf?

Here is a prayer to recite when "Wrestling With **Anochi.**" The language is interwoven, for it speaks simultaneously to the transcendent **Anochi, I-Source**, and to **Anochi Within.**

From the fires of my anger,
from the pain of my bitter disappointment,
and from the depths of my despair,
I cry out:

*"Why, **Anochi**, Why?*
How long must I suffer?
How long must my spirit be crushed?"

And a Voice calls:
"Come into the cleft of the Rock;
Stand at the hardest of all places;
Look to the narrows of your soul.
And you will find Me there.

Struggle.
Wrestle.
Prevail.

In the fierceness of My embrace,
the narrows will widen.

Your wounds will be bound up;
Your shattered heart will be healed;
Your life-force will be restored;
And you will rise in wisdom."

And, so it is.

WD

ANOCHI-LIKE

Being in Never-Ending **Anochi**-Love

The real name of God, **Anochi**—the transcendent God and the **God Within**—holds the quintessential purpose of **Anochi's** presence in our universe, and the reason that **Anochi** has created human beings and revealed **AnochiSelf** to us.

Moses asks of **Anochi**, "Please show me Your glory" (Exodus 33:18).

> *What is **Anochi**'s glory?*
> *Love.*
> *Anochi is Love—pure Love.*
> *And **Anochi** created us to be Love—pure Love.*

Sometimes we ignore what we know; sometimes we forget. Sometimes we let the little annoyances of life—and what we think are the big issues of life—get in our way, so that we are no longer conscious of the greatness and the power of **Anochi's** Love, and ours.

Anochi's name has been found at this moment in time—when, in so many ways, the fate of our universe teeters in the balance—so that **Anochi's** message of Love can "fill the Earth as the waters fill the sea" (after Habbakuk 2:14).

Since the exile from Eden, the split of the Divine Masculine and the Divine Feminine has been paradigmatic of all the diverse (and often dichotomous) elements in our world and in ourselves: darkness and light, justice and mercy, war and peace, hatred and love.

Our Earth desperately needs our help to end the division, to bring an end to the strife and conflict, to restore the balance, and to weave the harmony, so that Love can triumph. Our **Anochi Within** must act. We are the Earth-weavers who can braid together the diversity—beginning with that which was first shattered—the masculine and the feminine.

Knowing that the masculine aspect of God is called YHWH (*Adonai*), and that the feminine aspect of God is called *Shechinah*, we can call out to *Adonai* and *Shechinah* in this antiphonal request, "Braiding the Divine Masculine and the Divine Feminine." Everyday, if you can, speak each verse in order, alternately addressing *Adonai* and *Shechinah*. When you come to the last two verses, **Anochi** is the synthesizer. At the conclusion of the prayer, chant "**Anochi**" and "I Love You," in the quiet meditative melody.

Your prayer will go out to the universe, and together we will help build up the mass of energy that will move the world to healing.

As **Anochi** is Whole and One, we can strive to be Whole and One.

1. **ADONAI**, would You please lift up Your heart to our hearts and spirits?
2. **SHECHINAH**, would You please attune Your heart to our hearts and spirits?
3. **ADONAI**, would You please traverse the ages to be here now?
4. **SHECHINAH**, would You please embrace the ages to be here now?
5. **ADONAI**, would You please shine the light of holiness on us?
6. **SHECHINAH**, would You please reflect the light of compassion in us?
7. **ADONAI**, would You please enable the righting of the Tree of Knowledge to stand in alignment with the Tree of Life?
8. **SHECHINAH**, would You please enable the Tree of Life to accept the righting of the Tree of Knowledge?
9. **ADONAI**, would You please remember the ones who hold steadfast the vision of redemption?
10. **SHECHINAH**, would You please accept the ones who hold steadfast the shadow of doubt?
11. **ADONAI**, would You please build consciousness with grace and joy?
12. **SHECHINAH**, would You please support consciousness with kindness and gratitude?
13. **ADONAI**, would You please dream us returning to Paradise?
14. **SHECHINAH**, would You please deliver us into transcendent beauty?
15. **ADONAI**, would You please send forth the song of creation into these universes?

16. **SHECHINAH**, would You please receive the song of creation, and sing it to Your children?

17. **ADONAI**, would You please invite the ones in whom You delight to the recitation?

18. **SHECHINAH**, would You please make welcome those in whom You delight?

19. **ADONAI**, would You please redeem union from the surroundings of inequality?

20. **SHECHINAH**, would You please bless union with the surroundings of connection?

21. **ADONAI**, would You please plant the intention of form?

22. **SHECHINAH**, would You please enwomb the substance of life?

23. **ADONAI**, would You please contain the Heart of Paradise, so that return is in our hearts?

24. **SHECHINAH**, would You please increase the Heart of Paradise, so that return is now?

25. **ADONAI**, would You please join with **THE SHECHINAH** to make a New World?

26. **SHECHINAH**, would You please return from separation to make a New World?

27. **ADONAI**, would You please engage **THE SHECHINAH** in sacred marriage?

28. **SHECHINAH**, would You please engage **ADONAI** in sacred marriage?

29. **ANOCHI**, would You please At-One us with Your radiance, so that we may reflect You?

30. **ANOCHI**, would You please At-One us with Your radiance, so that we may reflect You?

Now, chant

ANOCHI
I LOVE YOU

WD & ELKD

To hear the Anochi - I Love You chant, visit www.GodisAnochi.com

Anochi is Love. You are Love. The person next to you is Love. The person across the world is Love. The people with whom there is conflict are Love. The nations with whom there is war are Love. The places where there is hatred, or darkness or fear, are Love.

By having **Anochi's** real name, the eternal truth is remembered and affirmed: All is Love. Love is All.

How do we best let **Anochi** in? How do we best experience **Anochi's** Love?

> See, feel, experience **Anochi** above pouring enormous, infinite, unending Love down into you.
> Let your heart be open to receive all of it.
> And when you think that your heart is as open as it can be, open it even more—and let **Anochi's** Love pour in.
> And when you are so full of **Anochi's** Love that you are overflowing with it, open your heart even further, and let all that Love flow through you . . . and out through your open heart to the whole world—every place and space, every inch of it.
> And leave your heart open, and **Anochi's** Love pouring through.
>
> ELKD

To celebrate **Anochi's** infinite love for you, and your overflowing love for **Anochi**, you can chant the words *Ahavah Rabbah,* "With Greatest Love," and *Ahavat Olam,* "Eternal Love."

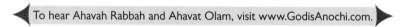

To hear Ahavah Rabbah and Ahavat Olam, visit www.GodisAnochi.com.

STAYING WITH **ANOCHI**

Being in Never-Ending **Anochi**-Light

Now that we know God's real name, now that we can know **Anochi** in wholeness and Oneness, we can stay in **Anochi's** Holy Presence—both the transcendent Presence and the presence within—everywhere, all the time.

When Moses came down the mountain, he was bathed in God's Light; he was beaming with God's Light.[16] That holy Light reflected onto everyone Moses met.

How do you get and sustain the glorious feeling of being "in the Light," in **Anochi's** Holy Presence; how do you continually illumine **Anochi Within**?

Stay with **Anochi**.

Embrace **Anochi Within**.

The Jewish tradition is to say one hundred blessings a day.[17]

St. Paul taught, "Pray always."[18]

The Chasidic Rebbe Nachman of Bratslav said, "Pray. Pray. Pray."[19]

One hundred blessings a day? Pray always? Pray, pray, pray?

How is that possible? There would not be time for anything else.

Metaphoric though it may be, that, of course, is the point.

If you say a blessing now, and know that you are to say a blessing five minutes from now; if you pray now, and know that you are soon to be praying again, then, you stay with **Anochi**. **Anochi** stays with you and within you.

> When you call to Me, and come, and pray to Me,
> I will hear you.
> When you seek Me, you will find Me,
> if you search for Me with all your heart.
> I shall let you find Me.
>
> —JEREMIAH 29:12–13

In constant **Anochi**-Light, it is hard to say an unkind word, to be discourteous, to cheat in business, to tell a lie. When you are with **Anochi**, and **Anochi** is Within you, you are certainly aware of **Anochi's** word; you continue to do **Anochi's** will.

When you pray always, when you talk to **Anochi** always, when you say one hundred blessings a day, you stay in the flow of **Anochi's** design; you stay at-One with **Anochi**. You stay in your own **Anochi-ness**. You affirm **Anochi Within**.

So, be in **Anochi**-Energy; stay in **Anochi's** Light and Love. Eventually, every moment can be an **Anochi** moment.

Be like Moses: Be beamed with **Anochi's** Light, and become a beam of **Anochi's** Light; let **Anochi Within** shine forth.

To remind yourSelf how to stay with **Anochi**, how to be in the Holy Presence—how your **Anochi Within** *is* the Holy Presence— you can say this prayer-intention, which speaks your intention to yourSelf.

I now have one hundred percent desire that blessing open the ways that I walk.
   so that I Am surrounded with the fulfillment of my heart's desires.
     Now and ForEver, there is a converging of
       Eternal Time and
         Infinite Space and
          my Being
     so that the Wisdom of ForEver and AllWays is my true Point of Light.

I now have one hundred percent desire that blessing flows through me,
   and saturates this World,
     so that I Am filled with Faith, and Trust, and Hope.

ELKD

To remember **Anochi's** Light in you, and your Light shining out to the world, you can chant this verse from the Psalms (36:10) *"B'OrChah nir-eh Or"*—"In Your Light, we see Light."

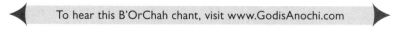
To hear this B'OrChah chant, visit www.GodisAnochi.com

Now and always, give your **Anochi**-Light to everyone you meet.

REFLECTING **ANOCHI**
Being in Never-Ending **Anochi**-Energy

The writer-philosopher Aldous Huxley[20] teaches that everything— everything—is a manifestation of the Divine. We know that the elephant, and the orange, and the tree, and the rock, and the but-terfly, and you, and your child, and your next-door neighbor, and the stranger on the street, and the unknown one across the world, are all of God.

And we know, as the philosopher maintains, that human life has but one purpose: to identify with your Eternal Self, your **Anochi-I, Anochi Within**, and to come into unitive knowledge of the Divine. That is, we all exist, we live, for one reason: to know God.

All of life—all that we think, know, experience, and feel—begins with an idea, **Anochi's** or ours. Thus, all of life is a combination of reason and faith—knowing and believing, scholarly inquiry, and sacred spirit.

To remember and celebrate that this is "true and certain,"[21] you can chant *"Emet V'Emunah kol zot"*—"Faith and Reason are All That Is."

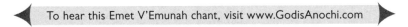
To hear this Emet V'Emunah chant, visit www.GodisAnochi.com

When you shine your **Anochi Within** Light—your God-ness—outward, it reflects off everything and everyone you see.

You become like a mirror. You open to others, who shine their **Anochi Within** Light—their God-ness—onto you, and, then, it reflects back to them.

In another, you no longer see "The Other," but you begin to see **Anochi**. It is **Anochi Within** seeing **Anochi Within**.

It is your embrace of the Hindu energy of "Namaste"—the God within me acknowledges the God within you; my GodSelf honors your GodSelf.

And you begin to see the unity, the Oneness, of all.

Sometimes, it is easy to forget that the teller in the bank who seems to take forever to complete a transaction, or the young clerk in the store who has trouble making change, or the driver who rudely cuts you off in traffic, is of God.

Sometimes—most times—it is easy to forget that the ideologue who opposes you, the terrorist who strikes out at you, the general who makes war against you, the fundamentalist who threatens your very existence, is of God.

Their God-Light seems to be very dim; their **Anochi Within** seems to be absent or lost.

But, when you are able to stay aware and be conscious of the God-ness of every One, you remember that there is really no separation between you and **Anochi**, *and* there is really no separation between you and every other human being.

As Rabbi Danya Ruttenberg writes in her book, *Surprised by God,*[22] quoting her college friend Alex, who became an Episcopalian priest: ". . . eventually you run up against the heightened awareness that the person cleaning your office building is tired, is human, that somehow you are responsible for her being there since 4 a.m., which is not a comfortable awareness."

Your **Anochi Within** energy can be a celebration for those who, like you, strive to be ever-consciousness of the Divine. And your **Anochi Within** energy can be a reflective beacon for those who deny—or some-times fail to see—theirs.

Then, you can do your part to move the world away from separation and closer to unity.

How can there possibly be abject poverty in this world? How can there be oppressive hunger? How can there be lack of potable water? How can there be rampant disease? How can there be illiteracy? How can there be war?

These social, cultural, and geopolitical horrors exist because we forget to give our **Anochi Within** energy on to others, and to take in **Anochi Within** energy from those who give to us. Our GodSelves forget—or ignore—the **God Within**.

And so, we challenge ourselves with the wisdom of the ages: "Remember. Do not forget" (Deuteronomy 25:17–19).

Within rich and precious differences, there is Oneness.

Within every human being, there is **Anochi**.

To help you remember your God-ness, the **God Within**, you can say this little prayer attributed to Rabbi Levi Yitzchak of Berditchev.[23] This version is a combination of a number of translations, and has been adapted to address **Anochi**. Reb Levi Yitzchak was speaking to the transcendent God, **Anochi, I-Source**, the God of the Heavens above. He could just as well have been speaking to the **Anochi-I**, the **God Within** you, and—to remind you—that God is also within every human being.

Anochi, Anochi:
Let me sing You a song
my You-song to You.
You, You, You,
You, You, You!

For there, where I go—You!
And here, where I Am—You!
When I Am glad—You!
And when I Am sad—You!
Only You, just You,
always You—and You again.
You, You, You
You, You, You!

East is You, West is You,
North is You, South is You.
Sky is You! Earth is You!
You Above! You Below!
Only You.
You, You, You.

On every path, at every end,
only You, just You.
Always You,
And You again.
You, You, You!
You, You, You!

ANOCHI EVERLASTING

Being in Never-Ending **Anochi**-Life

An old legend teaches that at the moment of Creation, **Anochi** created every soul that would ever, ever be.[24]

And, every soul is eternal; it exists forever and ever.

Most of the time, souls reside with **Anochi** in the Heavens; sometimes souls go on mission to other realms; sometimes souls come to Earth, animate a body, and live as a human being.

Most souls that come to Earth are very glad to be here. Earth is a wonderful place of exploration, growth, and soul satisfaction.

Yet, some souls are not so pleased to leave the paradise of the Heavens. They do not want to leave the proximity of being in the Holy Presence, and staying "warm" with **Anochi**. They do not want to follow the "rules" that require having to give up holding eternal knowledge during life on Earth. They consider being birthed on Earth as a passing over, a passing away, a dying from the world of perfection to a less desirable world of striving and strife.

Either happily or somewhat reluctantly, for however long a soul is in an Earth-body—just Earth-moments, or ninety or one hundred twenty Earth-years—it embraces and clings to life with fierce determination. For some souls, life in an Earth-body is sweet and good. For others, it is bewildering and painful. For all, it is challenging.

Yet—whatever the situation or circumstance—the life force, and the love of life, and the determination to stay alive, is always strong and powerful.

So, when the time comes for a soul's journey on this Earth to end, most souls are reluctant to leave. Yet, just as every soul came from being with **Anochi**, every soul returns to be with **Anochi**. So, when **Anochi** takes away our breath and our animation, it is said that a soul passes over, passes away, dies. But, it does not fade into the nothingness of oblivion. A soul leaves this Earth and passes over right back to the Heavenly realms. With a whoosh of sudden swiftness, or a long, slow, ever-diminishing soft whisper, **Anochi, I-Source** withdraws Divine breath from our being, and our once life-animated Earth-body becomes an empty vessel. The spirit of **Anochi** continually abides in our eternal soul. Our soul lives in the Infinite **Anochi**: always, and forever.

How the body from spirit does unwind / Until we are pure spirit at the end.[25]

A soul is eternal—whether in Heaven or Earth. A soul is eternal—with **Anochi** always.

When someone we love—or when we—die from this Earth, we are often sad and bereft, because the bonds that love created seem severed. Yet, love is eternal; "Love is as strong as death" (Song of Songs 8:6). The bonds of love are eternal.

The veil between this side and the other side is growing thinner and thinner. Our human consciousness is becoming more and more aware of what our soul consciousness has always known: that wherever we are—here or there—we are with **Anochi**, always and forever.

The part of the soul that is constant—whether in Heaven or on Earth, in life or in death—is **Anochi Within**.

Anochi Within is the spark within our souls that gives our souls life—in any realm—and makes our souls eternal. It is that which holds eternal, universal knowledge. It is the place where Heaven and Earth touch; the most intimate merging of eternal lovers at the point of being, the Point of Essence. It is always and forever.

Anochi Within, our everlasting soul, is the awesome place of revelation and knowing, redemption and salvation, transformation and evolution, grace and harmony, peace and love.

Anochi Within, our everlasting soul, is Oneness with **Anochi**.

To be consciously aware of and rejoice in your eternal soul and in life eternal, you can chant *Chai-ei-Olam B'Nafshi*—"In my Soul is Life Eternal."

To hear this Chai-ei-Olam, visit www.GodisAnochi.com

To affirm and celebrate **Anochi** Everlasting—**Anochi, I-Source**, and **Anochi-I, Anochi Within**, on this side and the other side, you can chant *"Anochi Tamid"*—"**Anochi** All-Ways/All-Ways **Anochi**."[26]

To hear this Anochi Tamid chant, visit www.GodisAnochi.com

OPENING TO **ANOCHI**

Being with **Anochi**

To rejoice in **Anochi Within** you; to affirm the deepest love that you and **Anochi** share; to proclaim the Oneness of **Anochi** and of all **Anochi's** worlds and creatures; to hasten a time when—on Earth and in the Heavens—it is Eden once again; every time it feels right and good, say this affirming prayer for "Opening to **Anochi**."[27]

> I fully open my heart to be in **Anochi's** Heart.
> I fully open my love to be in **Anochi's** Love.
> I fully open my soul to be in **Anochi's** Perfection.
> I fully open my being to be in **Anochi's** Oneness.
> "I Am That I Am."

At this deepest, deepest place of connection, this is where you meet **Anochi, I-Source** and **Anochi, I** *Panim el Panim,* "Face to Face."

To guide you on your way, you can sing the powerful chant—*Panim el Panim,* "Face to Face"—from the "Inside of the Insides."

◄ To hear this Panim el Panim chant, visit www.GodisAnochi.com ►

WHO KNOWS ONE?

———◄◦►———

An old story—updated for our time:

High in the mountains was a retreat center that had once been known throughout the world. The men and women who lived here were spiritual seekers; the people who came on retreat were enthusiastic. The chanting, and praying, and meditating deeply touched the hearts of all who came there.

But, something had changed. Fewer and fewer young women and men came to join the center; fewer and fewer people came for spiritual nourishment. Those who remained were disheartened and sad.

Deeply worried, the spiritual guide of the center went off in search of an answer. Why had the retreat center fallen on such hard times?

The guide came to an old sage, and asked, "Is it because of some fault of ours, some sin of ours, that our center has fallen on such hard times?"

"Yes," replied the sage. "It is because of the sin of ignorance."

"The sin of ignorance?" questioned the guide. "Of what are we ignorant?"

The sage looked at the guide for a long, long time, and then said, "One of you is the messiah in disguise. But you are all ignorant of this." The sage—as always happens in stories like this—then was silent.

"The messiah?" thought the guide. "The messiah one of us? Impossible." But, the sage had spoken. And, so, the guide considered:

Who could it be? Is it Brother Cook? Is it Sister Vegetable Grower? Is it Brother Treasurer? Is it Sister Bell Ringer?

"Which one? Which one? We all have our faults, our flaws, our failings. Isn't the messiah supposed to be perfect? But, then, maybe the faults and failings are part of a disguise. Which one? Which one?"

When the guide returned to the center, all the brothers and sisters gathered around, and the guide told them what the sage had said.

"One of us? The messiah? Impossible."

But, the sage had spoken, and the sage was never wrong.

One of us? The messiah? Incredible! But, it must be so. Which one? Which one? That brother over there? That sister? That one? That one? Which one? Which one?

Whichever of the brothers and sisters it was, the messiah was, surely, in disguise.

So, not knowing who amongst them was the messiah, they all began treating each other with new respect. Their words were sweeter; their actions toward each other were kinder. "You never know," each one thought. "He might be the one; she might be the one. I had better treat each and every one with decency and dignity, with grace and honor."

And—as always happens in stories like this—it was not long before the center was filled with newfound joy. Soon, new young men and women came to live and learn there; people came from far and wide to be inspired by the smiles and the kindness that filled the center. Even the vegetables tasted better. Even the bells seemed to sound happy.

For, once again, the center was filled with the spirit of love.

◆○◆

The Sage teaches:

"We are God's stake in human history. We are the day and the dusk, the challenge and the test."[1]

EIGHT

ANOCHI'S PROMISE

אָנֹכִי אָנֹכִי אָנֹכִי

THE DAYS ARE COMING

In the prophetic section of the Bible, **Anochi** invokes the image of the prophet Elijah, who according to tradition will be the one to announce the coming of the messianic time of love and peace on Earth:

> Behold, **Anochi, I-Source** will send you Elijah the prophet—the coming of that great and awesome day.   —MALACHI 3:23

No aspect of Source, no representative God, will suffice. **Anochi, I-Source** will send the herald to bring the return of total perfection and pure love, the paradise of Eden on Earth.

From a childhood image, I call that place "Sky Blue," the very, very best place we and our world can be.[1]

There, we will joyfully understand that **Anochi, I-Source** is waiting for us—to speak the Name, to serve the Name, and to be the Name.

There, we will joyfully understand that **Anochi-I, Anochi Within** is waiting for us—to recognize and embrace and celebrate.

Just as this book is being completed, highly spiritually attuned people all across the globe are experiencing a budding awareness of the beginnings of an extraordinary phenomenon.

An old legend teaches that in the beginning—before the beginning—

Anochi's Light filled the entire universe. In order to make space for all that was to be created, **Anochi, I-Source** breathed in, withdrawing some of the Divine Light, thus making place for all that was to be created.

The mystics called this withdrawal *tzimtzum*—literally: "contraction."

Now, at this very moment in time—for only the second time in recorded history—another **Anochi**-*tzimtzum* is taking place. Yet, this *tzimtzum* is significantly different from the first. Then, **Anochi** contracted **Anochi's** Light to make room for creation. Now, **Anochi**—who infuses all creation—is contracting some of **AnochiSelf** from some of that creation.

Why?

The brokenness of our world, the massive effects on humankind of the events of nature, the breakdown of so many national and geopolitical monetary and societal systems, and—particularly—the revolutions for human freedom that are being staged by the young people of the world, mean that creation as we have known it is being destroyed and swept away. Monumental change is coming in the world order. A New World is birthing—free of old long-held impediments and fears that have kept us from full spiritual consciousness and connection.

In order to make space for this enormous change, **Anochi, I-Source** is contracting some of **AnochiSelf** for a predetermined amount of time for the specific purpose of making room for this New Creation.

So, what are we supposed to do in the meantime? How are we to function during this *tzimtzum*?

Because our external world is shifting so rapidly, and it seems as if there is nothing solid or secure to hang onto, we are to get in deep touch with our internal world, our **Anochi-I, Anochi Within.** We know that within each and every one of us is the fullness of God, because we know **Anochi** "from the Insides of the Insides." Within each and every one of us is the wisdom, and the discernment, and the strength, and the compassion, and the friendship, and the love to shape and forge the new world, to bring **Anochi**-consciousness to our lives.

Anochi, I-Source is saying to us, "My children, My co-creating partners, it is our world together. As this world changes, remember: everything you need to bring our world to full spiritual consciousness and greatest Love is within you. When you energize your **Anochi Within**, your **GodSelf**, to the heights and depths of your potential, to the core of your spiritual being, you are sure to bring about the long-ago promise of the coming of Elijah, and the reality of Eden on Earth once again."

To be in fullest connection with your **Anochi Within**, you can say this powerful and beautiful affirmation. After saying each phrase, breathe deeply. At the conclusion of the affirmation, breathe deeply three times.

> I Am flowing with well-being.
> I Am experiencing life.
> I Am renewing what has been restrained.
> I Am manifesting balance.
> I Am becoming the flowering of Humankind.
> I Am the Center.
> I Am Bringing Heaven on Earth.
> I Am acknowledged as the Being of Magnificence That I Am.
> "I Am That I Am."[2]

You can now joyously chant: "Elijah, the Prophet, Bring Sky Blue Now!"

◄ To hear this Elijah chant, visit www.GodisAnochi.com ►

ONE NAME

Anochi is the One name for God that can be recognized, accepted, and embraced by Judaism, Christianity, and Islam—the three major religions that revere the Hebrew Bible, and source themselves in the faith of Abraham—and can be acknowledged and appreciated by all peoples of the Earth.

Children have individual, unique names for their parents—Mom or Mommy; Dad or Pop—just as Jews, Christians, and Muslims—and all people of faith and spirit—have individual, unique names for God (*Adonai,* Jesus, *Allah*).

Jews, Christians, and Muslims will keep their own names for God, but at the same time we now have the One name of God that is not suffused with any individually charged religious or political implication and certainly not with any parochial triumphalism.

We now have one name that we can all comfortably and gratefully call the One Father/Mother God—**Anochi, I-Source.**

That is why, at this moment in time, meeting **Anochi** is so awesome and exciting.

That is why, at this moment in time, touching **Anochi-I, Anochi Within** is so fulfilling and soul satisfying.

It is the prelude to all God's children touching hands in peace.

For, then, in the words of the modern poet, Judy Chicago,

> *. . . All that has divided us will merge*
> *And then compassion will be wedded to power*
> *And then softness will come to a world that is harsh and*
> *   unkind*
> *And then both men and women will be gentle*
> *And then both women and men will be strong*
> *And then no person will be subject to another's will*
> *And then all will be rich and free and varied*
> *And then the greed of some will give way to the needs of*
> *   many*
> *And then we will all share equally in the Earth's*
> *   abundance*
> *And then all will care for the sick and the weak and the old*
> *And then all will nourish the young*
> *And then all will cherish life's creatures*
> *And then all will live in harmony with each other and with*
> *   the Earth*
> *And then everywhere will be called Eden once again*[3]

And, then, in beautiful song, you can chant some of these words to envision—and participate in—our world evolving into a place of goodness and right.

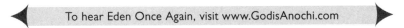

To hear Eden Once Again, visit www.GodisAnochi.com

And, then, on a great and awesome day, we will all know and proclaim:

> **Anochi** is One.
> **Anochi's** Name is One.
> The world is One.
> We, **Anochi's** children—all of us together—are One.
>
> And then, in grand jubilation, **Anochi** will declare,
> "In the new beginning. . . ."

To wrap yourSelf in this vision and promise of Oneness, chant: "One God. One World. One People. Eden on Earth."

To hear this One God chant, visit www.GodisAnochi.com

THE ULTIMATE WORD

Through the prophet Jeremiah, **Anochi, I-Source** speaks the ultimate and definitive word:

> You shall be My people, and **Anochi, I-Source** will be [in the office of] your *Elohim* [your God].   —JEREMIAH 30:22

And, from the depths of **Anochi-I, God Within**, we human beings reply:

> **Anochi-I** observed and took it to heart. I saw it and learned.
>   —PROVERBS 24:32

And,

> May my prayer be pleasing to Him [God]. **Anochi-I** will rejoice. . . .
>   —PSALMS 104:34

NINE

THE AFFIRMATION

To affirm your ongoing and everlasting faith in **Anochi**, your commitment to **Anochi**, and your love for **Anochi**, whenever and wherever it feels right and good, you can chant this affirmation:[1]

ברוך שם יחידות הָאָנֹכִי לְעוֹלם לְעוֹלם וָעֶד

*Baruch Shem Yichudut **HA-ANOCHI**, L'Olam L'Olam Va'ed*

Because this is a ritualistic blessing, we use the definitive article *Ha*—THE—to indicate the One and only **Anochi**.

"Blessed is the Name and the Oneness of **Anochi**, Now and Forever, Forevermore."

◀ To hear this Affirmation chant, visit www.GodisAnochi.com ▶

ANOCHI, ANOCHI

Return me unto You, **Anochi**,
And I will return.
Renew my days
as at the very, very Beginning.

I come from **Anochi**.
I "strut and fret my hour upon the stage."
And, then,
I return to **Anochi**, who is my Home.

From **Anochi**.
To **Anochi**.
Always, in the Light of **Anochi**.
The circle is never-ending.
The circle continues still.
Blessed Am I in my coming in.
Blessed Am I in my going out.

Wherever I Am,
I Am with **Anochi**,
Anochi is with me.
Anochi is Within me.

Blessed Am I.
Blessed Am I.
I Am greatly blessed.

Anochi. Anochi. Anochi.
I come to know You—in all Your awesome glory.
I come to know You—in all Your wondrous works.
I come to know You—in the breath of my being.
I come to know You—in the depths of my soul.

*You are **Anochi**.*
You are my God.
From the beginning.
*You are **Anochi**.*
Forever and ever.
*You are **Anochi**.*
You enwrap me in covenantal love.
You guide me with providential grace.

In the Heavens and on Earth,
I Am Yours.
In the ever-unfolding works of Creation,
I Am Yours.
In the innermost of my heart,
And in the Heart of Hearts,
I Am Yours.
In the ever-continuing journey back to Eden,
I Am Yours.
In Life and in Life-Everlasting,
I Am Yours.

Anochi. Anochi. Anochi.
I love You. I love You. I love You.

I offer You myriad thanks.
I exalt You in manifold praise.
I revel in You deep Inside.

With perfect faith, I believe:
*I dwell forever in **Anochi's** House.*
***Anochi** is my hope and my promise.*
***Anochi** is my goodness and my righteousness.*
***Anochi** is my Light and my salvation.*
I Am ever-glad and ever-grateful.

Only one thing do I ask.
This do I desire:
*Bless me, **Anochi**,*
Please bless me
In the Light of Your Holy Presence.
And under the Wings of Your Enduring Love.
And may I,
I pray,
be a blessing to You.

The Eternal embrace remains forever sweet.
Because **Anochi** loves us—
all of us, together.[1]

A PERSONAL WORD

—◁○▷—

NOW I KNOW that the biblical YHWH—*Adonai* of Hebrew Scripture and Jewish prayer is not God, but only an aspect of God.

Now I know that **Anochi** is the whole, complete God, the Full Essence of God.

So what does this discovery do for my relationship with God, for the place of my religion, Judaism—its beliefs, practices, people, culture, land, destiny—in my life, and the lives of those I continue to serve as rabbi and teacher? What does it do for my own faith?

What does it do for Judaism and the Jewish people, for Christians, and Muslims, for people of all religions and of no religion, of all faiths and of no faith?

What does it mean for the contemporary counterpoint between "religion" and "spirituality," for the disagreements within individual religious communities, for the ongoing tensions between various religious and faith communities?

And what does this discovery do for you?

A core, organizing principle of human life on our planet throughout the ages has been that identity is destiny.

Now we have learned that the core, foundational element of much of human belief and behavior—God—has been partially based on a case of mistaken identity.

God, surely, is God. Yet, the name(s) and many of the characteristics that we have attributed to God are only a part of God. Because we have not known the real name of God, we have not known the real, whole, complete full essence of God.

Now, we know God's real identity.

Now, we can know the whole, complete God.

While this discovery opens whole new worlds of thought and practice for us, do we somehow feel that our own identities are mistaken or compromised? Are our long-held truths and the long-established foundations of our whole lives no longer certain?

Our initial uneasiness can be happily mitigated when we rejoice in the enormity of what we have learned: Now, we know that God who is **Anochi** holds both genders; that **Anochi** is both the transcendent, supernatural God, and, at the same time, the intimate **God Within**; that **Anochi** is not solely a god of vengeful anger or revenge; that **Anochi** is One—the One God of all of us. "All souls are One. Each is a spark of the original Soul, and this Soul is inherent in all souls."[1]

And as we strive toward a world of peace and love, knowing **Anochi's** real identity also affirms our own identity—as children of the One, loving God—and can reshape our collective destiny into living the vision and promise: One God. One World. One People.

For me: Knowing what I now know about the biblical name of God, I can no longer be a YHWH-ist.

Having found **Anochi**, I have been given a modern-day revelation that answers my theological questions of mind, heart, and soul; that enriches and ennobles my spiritual practices and experiences; and that brings a settled, comfortable, joy-filled wholeness to my being.

I am an **Anochi-ist**.

I seek the full Essence of the Complete God.

I seek a deep, personal, intimate relationship with **Anochi**.

I seek to fully connect with **Anochi Within**, my GodSelf.

In practical terms: What am I?

I am passionately Jewish. I have a great appreciation for all forms of Judaism. I am equally comfortable—and equally uncomfortable—with most all forms of Jewish expression. I love Israel, and I feel deeply bound to all Jews everywhere. And, at the same time, I am a universal pluralist—respecting and honoring all religions and faiths.

In one story is every story, so perhaps your spiritual journey may be reflected in mine.

Sometimes, I like praying with a congregation. Yet, in the midst of a large communal gathering, I often find it hard to have a private, soulful conversation with God. Large crowds and a public prayer agenda are rarely conducive to intimate exchange.

So, I have developed a personal daily spiritual practice, where my chants, meditations, and deepest prayers are directed to the whole, complete God. Rooted in tradition, it is, for me, a direct (and brief) compelling, powerful, joyous, and very soul satisfying renewed pathway to a sweet and holy personal, intimate relationship with **Anochi**. (*For an introduction to this practice, please see my book,* 20-Minute Kabbalah.)

When I guide others in worship, I try to create holy space: a safe and sacred place for people to connect and communicate with **Anochi** by stepping into **Anochi-ness**. Viewing a picture hanging on a wall can be sublime, but stepping into the picture—as is possible with a diorama (which in elementary school art class we used to call a "shadow box") is to truly be with God, to cleave to God, to be in *yichud*—intimate, merged union. This prayer process was recently described: "The rabbi began to sing, and in the sweet songs was the invitation, 'Come in. Help yourself to God.'"

I love to learn traditional Jewish texts—both rational and mystical teachings. I look at a text for all its possibilities: its stories, history, theology, ritual and ethical law, social justice, politics, sociology, culture, and for the ways my ancestors found, encountered, and related to **Anochi**—and what all this means for my life, identity, and relationships.

My regard for Jewish ritual is a bit more complicated. I am uncomfortable with much of the Jewish holiday cycle that revolves around commemorations based on the theme: "Somebody tried to kill us; we won; let's eat." I am happy to celebrate survival, but too many of our holidays begin in the lament over what others tried to do to us. I am much happier with the holidays that rejoice in **Anochi**, and our mission in **Anochi's** world.

I remain uncomfortable with the traditional blessings that call YHWH, "the King," and focus on YHWH's commands. For me, the blessings I have rewritten—which appear earlier in this book—solve the problem by addressing **Anochi** as the "Source of all Worlds, and Breath/Spirit of all Living Beings," and praise **Anochi** who has "made us holy through grace and unconditional covenantal love, and enlivens/animates us."

I well understand ritual commands as the touchstones that bring us closer to God, so as I come closer and closer to **Anochi** through my own spiritual practice, I embrace the traditional ritual injunctions that still speak to me with their inherent power and worth, and I disregard (or continue through habit, or rote, or guilt) the commands that feel old, tired, and irrelevant. The deeper and deeper I come into intimate relationship with **Anochi**, the less and less I am personally concerned with ritual commands, and the more and more I feel connected through faith and love. And I am heartened by the teaching in the Talmud (Babylonian Talmud, *Nidah* 61b) that "ritual *mitzvot* [commandments] will be abolished [for they will be no longer necessary] when the Messiah comes."

Anochi's sublime and infinitely wise ethical commands still hold great power for me, and, I would contend, for our whole world. For, through the observance of the ethical commands—particularly acts of social justice and human loving-kindness—and through evolving human consciousness, and through the revelation of **Anochi's** true identity in our time, I believe that we are coming closer and closer to the messianic age of perfection—the time of healing and transformation, goodness and justice, faith and enlightenment, peace and love.

I love, love, love the Land of Israel, and, especially, the holy and eternal city of Jerusalem—the place of supreme holiness; the place where

Heaven and Earth touch. And, I am deeply pained by the ongoing—and devastating—conflict between Israel and her neighbors over recognition, defense, security, and peace.

Can there—will there—ever be the understanding, dialogue, and cooperation that will end the enmity, so that the children of Isaac and the children of Ishmael, the children of Jacob and the children of Esau, can finally touch hands in peace?

My dream is the eternal dream: Eden on Earth once again. Now, with the discovery of the whole, complete God, **Anochi**, our world is more and more ready for wholeness, the completeness, of perfection. As **Anochi's** co-creative partners, we know: The Garden awaits the gardeners. "With perfect faith, I believe"[2] that the time is near.

So: I am a rational Jewish thinker, trained in both the classical tradition, and in the methodology of academic, historic inquiry. *And* I am a Jewish spiritualist—an egalitarian neo-Kabbalist, coming to **Anochi** through holy intention, and an egalitarian neo-Chasid, coming to **Anochi** in great joy.

Am I part of, do I align with, any of the denominations of modern Judaism?

Yes—and, no.

Better, I am paradigmatic of the growing melding of the modern denominations.

If I am not yet completely "postdenominational," I am surely "transdenominational." Ultimately, I "bob and weave" among the many expressions of Judaism, because there is great validity and worth in everything Jewish.

So, that might make me a "Bob-er." But, there is a Chasidic sect named Bobover, and since it might be confusing, I cannot take that designation. And I cannot be a "Weaver," because there is really no "w" sound in Hebrew, so the name would be hard to pronounce.

Instead, I can dance with **Anochi**, and thus dance within and between denominations. And that works well for me—especially since I wrote a book entitled *Dancing with God* (now in its paperback edition called *Soul Judaism*)—because I can delicately swirl, and weave, and glide within all the modern expressions of Judaism and Jewish life.

The Hebrew word for "dance" is *rikkud*. I am, therefore, a "Rikkuder." That makes me the "Rikkuder Rebbe," promoting "Rukkudism Judaism."

Humor aside (or, maybe it is not so humorous after all) in many ways it seems that I am the face of the modern-day quest—of struggle and discovery—for all spiritual seekers.

As did the modern philosopher, Martin Buber, I seek "religion as Presence."[3] That is why in my book, *Dancing with God*, I name our contemporary, ever-evolving Judaism, *"Neshamah—Soul—Judaism,"* for our new Jewish expression will be most characterized by the return to the ever-possible reality of direct revelation, of personal prophecy, and by each person's deep, soulful, intimate relationship with **Anochi**. Whenever, wherever, and however **Anochi** calls, I come. I show up, and, like the prophet of old, I—you—say to the Infinite Presence, "Here I Am." And **Anochi** says, "I Am with you."[4]

At the same time, I am very well aware that if everyone takes a personal pathway to connection with **Anochi**, it may threaten to destroy the fabric of the community, for if each of us can come to **Anochi** alone, on our own personal spiritual quest and journey, what value is there in remaining part of the communal collective?

Frankly, that is an "old-energy" issue, because the inherent worth of community, and active involvement in it, has been long established. The "new-energy" question is: How do we best integrate the personal quest into the communal covenant? How do individual, intimate relationships with **Anochi** enrich and strengthen the collective whole?

Not to be trite, but as long as **Anochi** is the destination, the journey—on whatever pathways it takes us—can be quite a wondrous and miraculous revelatory adventure.

"In the deeper reality beyond space and time, we are all members of one body."[5]

In every faith community, similar questions are being asked; the quest, the searchings, the journeys, are much the same.

Who are we, and what are our lives?

At this moment, we all recognize that the fragility of our planet puts our common home at risk; the old forms of organizing our lives and our societies are crumbling and dying; a new world—sourced in Oneness Consciousness—is emerging. In fear of the unknown, and without inner resources to embrace the re-formation, religious and political zealots cling tight to their past. They attempt to keep our world from its spiritual evolution through their fundamentalism, extremism, terrorism, anti-Zionism, anti-Semitism, and anti-Americanism. Human beings who stand in **Anochi's** Light, men and women of peace and goodwill, are being sorely tested.

It used to be that the task of religious communities was to "hold the center" against rapid change, the momentarily popular, the trendy fad of the day. Now, it is the role of faith communities to be at the forefront of the "spiritual evolution-revolution"—introducing **Anochi**, advocating for **Anochi**, being **Anochi's** partners in bringing the reality of **Anochi** Consciousness and Oneness Consciousness to the world. Religion can no longer be the defender of what was, without being the passionate inspirer and mover into what will be.

The Jewish world is rife with conflict between the Orthodox and the liberals. Orthodox Jews are sourced in the unequivocal belief in the Divine authorship of Torah and the primacy of Torah law, while liberal Jews consider Jewish law to be open to the realities and re-interpretations of modernity. This fundamental divide leads to widely differing practices and observances, and serious dispute over matters of personal status, such as Jewish identity, marriage, divorce, and conversion.

At the same time, Israeli Jewry centers its life around what some term "secular Zionism"—the Jewish land, language, literature, calendar, holidays, and culture, but, except for a small minority, not religious beliefs or practice. In America, where there is high assimilation and acculturation, high rates of interfaith marriage, and low birth rate, there is nevertheless a continuing commitment to peoplehood, sparks of religious renewal and revival, tremendous excitement and vitality in academic and popular scholarship, communication in all its emerging technological forms, major creativity in the vast array of arts and culture, and enduring responsibility to issues of social justice.

A new, unique Judaism—still exceedingly formless, fluid, and, certainly, as yet undefined—is developing and growing. Hint: To me, it sounds and feels like Rukkidism Judaism, sourced in and by *Neshamah*—Soul—Judaism.

The contemporary question is will we be able to follow the Talmudic teaching, "These *and* these are *both* the words of the Living God?" (Babylonian Talmud, *Ketubot* 61b). Or, perhaps (much like the results of the Christian Reformation) are the conflicts so great that there will eventually be two Judaisms: one "traditional," and one encompassing the entirety of the broad "liberal" spectrum? Only time—and either the fortitude to keep a broken family together despite keen differences, or the courage to envision and forge as yet unimagined designs—will tell.

In Christianity, the Catholic Church is also confronted by the didactic tension between ancient beliefs and practices and the siren songs of modernity. Issues of the role of women; human sexuality (celibacy, birth control, and abortion); personal behavior of priests; the power of the hierarchy; relationships with other faith communities; and the wealth of the Church in the face of the abject poverty of so many of its faithful; all call for immediate and compassionate resolution.

In the Protestant Christian denominations, the tension is between the evangelical fundamentalists and the modern liberals. This conflict spills outside the pews of the churches into the American political arena, where there is a serious attempt to influence secular social policy based on religious beliefs. At the same time, all Christians are seeking to define place and purpose in this confusing, ever-changing world, trying to balance the past with the future, and asking the questions of creative survival. This has led the late Bishop John Shelby Spong *zt"l* to write books like *Why Christianity Must Change or Die* and *A New Christianity for a New World: Why Traditional Faith is Dying & How a New Faith Is Being Born*.

The worldwide Muslim community is currently in the throes of inner turmoil, determining who will dominate: the moderate religious, who choose to be part of the modern world, or the right wing militant fundamentalists, who are separatists and readily become terrorists in their stated manifesto to destroy Israel, control the Middle East, and eventually take over the world under Islamic law.

For all of us, the questions are much the same: How do we balance our spiritual quest with the Earthly realities of deeply felt religious, ethnic, tribal, territorial, and institutional loyalties? How do we open our hearts to the disagreements within our own communities, and the stark differences with other faiths? How do we best fulfill **Anochi's** ethical mandate to honor every human being as a child of **Anochi**, and to continually elevate the human condition and the human spirit?

And, in very practical arenas of religious belief and worship and education and ritual and observance: How do we stay relevant and energized to our principles and to our people? If there is a rejection of form or affiliation, how do we convey the sublime beauty and worth of our ancient traditions, and, at the same time, respond to modernity's sensibilities, needs, technologies, and openings? How do we avoid assimilation and giving up too much of our uniqueness, yet how do we avoid isolating so much that we shrivel up and fade away?

And always, always: How do we nourish the hunger for the sacred, the timeless, the interwoven, infinite connection?

As so often happens, most all of the answers lie within the questions themselves.

Hint: Most everything we do is empty and hollow unless **Anochi** is at the center. "Holy, holy, holy is **Anochi**" (Isaiah 6:3).

Another: "We have met the enemy, and it is us."[6] We need to be holy.

Another: The recognition of **Anochi** as God, and the embracing of **Anochi Within**, coupled with this new age of egalitarianism, means that the hierarchical structure of most communal institutions will give way to the circular—or better, the spiral—model, where wisdom is everywhere and everyone is wise. In the "new energy," new forms of worship, and learning, and communal loyalties emerge as much from the "user" as from the "provider." Holy sparks are everywhere.

"Bidden or unbidden,"[7] **Anochi**-energy, **Anochi**-consciousness, and **Anochi**-Presence is "bubbling up" and infusing minds and hearts.

More and more, those of all faiths who choose to embrace a spiritual life and lifestyle will do so not by habit or rote, from familial obligation, nostalgia, or guilt, but by happy engagement with **Anochi**—by feeling a palpable and growing sense of involvement, exhilaration, personal satisfaction, spiritual renewal, and sacred mission. Holy sparks ignite an as-yet-unimagined response.

Many contend that, throughout the millennia, the differences between religious beliefs, practices, and communities have been responsible for terrible divisiveness and destruction in our world. And, indeed, much human suffering, devastation, and death has been perpetrated in the "name of religion."

Now, all of us who trace our roots to the biblical Abraham—and that is all of us who are Jews, Christians, and Muslims, and many others with us—know that **Anochi** is our One common God, and that **Anochi** fills every heart with love, and calls all children to harmonious, peaceful, and joyful Oneness.

As **Anochi** makes known more of **AnochiSelf**, and as we all grow in wisdom by more fully connecting with **Anochi Within**, our differences will give way to our singular Source and our shared, mutual purposes; the mysteries will unfold, we will understand more and more, and the answers to our ardent searchings will be revealed. "Invisible lines of connection"[8] weave webs and networks of unity and interdependence. "A single Spirit fills infinity."[9]

That is why our evolving human consciousness has now brought us to this place of finding **Anochi**—the totality, the completeness, the Full Essence of God.

Anochi wants every human being on this Earth to know the fullness of **Anochi**, so that we who are "created in the Image of **Anochi**" will be like **Anochi**—totally open and accepting, fully embracing, and completely loving.

And I sense that as much as we want to know and be with **Anochi**, **Anochi** wants to be with us. **Anochi** yearns for a return to that time when **Anochi**, **AnochiSelf**, strolled in the Garden in the cool evening breeze, and exchanged pleasant greetings with all who wandered by.

Anochi eagerly awaits our full embrace.

I Am Wayne Dosick.
I Am a child of the universe.
I Am a child of **Anochi**.
"I Am that I Am."
And I celebrate my identity—and my destiny—in gratitude and gladness.

*And the Name of **Anochi***
rises up out of the song of Creation,
ripples into every crevice of time, place, and being,
and sweetly echoes across the face of Eternity.
And so it is.

CK & WD[10]

APPENDIX I

A SAMPLING

OF **ANOCHI** TEXTS IN

PROPHETS AND WRITINGS

The second and third sections of the Hebrew Bible are Prophets and Writings. Together, in Hebrew, they are called *Nach,* an acronym taken from the first letter (and sound) of each section's Hebrew name—*Nevi'im* (Prophets) and *Ketuvim* (Writings.)

Nach contains the history of the Jewish people from the entrance into the Promised Land of Israel, in approximately 1200 BCE, through the period of the Judges, the Kings, the building of the Holy Temple, the split of the kingdoms, the teachings and admonitions of the Prophets, the destruction of the Holy Temple (in 586 BCE), the exile to Babylonia, and the return some fifty years later. It also contains books of sublime Wisdom Literature, and books of historical recapitulation.

Even though the books of *Nach* are so diverse, and span well more than seven hundred years of ever-challenging, ever-changing history, the real name of God—**Anochi**—remains in use, and consistent in purpose and meaning when: 1) in God's voice, the wholeness and full essence of Source brings a message from God's GodSelf; and, 2) when in human voice, a person is expressing the fullness of his/her own GodSelf, **God Within**. Often, we encounter God—**Anochi, I-Source**—and a human being—**Anochi-I**—in fascinating dialogue.

Here are a few examples of some of the most compelling and powerful **Anochi** texts from a variety of places, settings, and situations in *Nach*.

Until now, each has been commonly translated with the simple "I."

THE DIVINE VOICE

When Joshua is about to lead the Israelites from the desert, across the Jordan River and into the promised land, he is charged by the full GodSelf of **Anochi,** who is about to fulfill a long-ago promise.

> My servant Moses is dead. Prepare to cross the Jordan, together with all this people, into the land that **Anochi, I-Source** Am giving to the Israelites.   —JOSHUA 1:2

David was one of the greatest kings of Israel. From his youthful slaying of Goliath, to his bringing the Tabernacle to Jerusalem to establish the Holy City as the religious and political center of the land and the people Israel, to his writings of the sublime prayer-psalms, he was the much beloved and highly revered leader of his people. To this day, Jews say, "David, King of Israel, Lives Forever!"

Yet, David was a man with all the foibles, flaws, and failings of a human being.

In a most famous—and troublesome—story, David falls in love with Bathsheva, the beautiful wife of Uriah the Hittite, and impregnates her. When his plan to make it seem as if the child is actually Uriah's fails, David orders that Uriah be placed in the front line of the battle, where, predictably, Uriah is killed.

God is very displeased with David's behavior, and sends the prophet Nathan to the king with a parable, mirroring David's conduct. When the prophet asks the king what should be done with such a man, David replies, "As YHWH lives, the man who did this deserves to die!" (II Samuel 12:5).

Invoking the voice of **Anochi, I-Source**—who in full God-ness is enraged and deeply offended by King David's behavior (as God in God's wholeness is sure to be)—Nathan says to David, in one of the greatest denouncements in all literature:

> You are the man! Thus says YHWH, the God of Israel, "**Anochi, I-Source** anointed you king over Israel, and **Anochi, I-Source** rescued you from Saul. . . . Why then have you flouted the command of YHWH, and done what so displeases?"   —II Samuel 12:7, 9

A biblical prophet is not a soothsayer nor a fortune-teller, but a messenger. S/he hears, sees, envisions, and dreams the word and will of God, and gives it over to people. In most cases, the prophecy is admonition against faithlessness toward God, and the consequences for violation of God's commands. At the same time, it offers hope for repentance and return, and always holds out the promise of redemption.

It is **Anochi, I-Source** who gives the call to prophecy and the message that the prophet is to convey.

Through the prophets, **Anochi, I-Source** emphatically establishes **Anochi's** place in the lives of the people and in the world.

> Thus says YHWH your Redeemer, who formed you in the womb: "It is **Anochi, I-Source** [represented by YHWH] who made everything, who alone stretched out the Heaven, and, unaided, spread out the Earth."   —Isaiah 44:24

> It is **Anochi, I-Source** who made the Earth and the men and beasts who are upon the Earth; by My great might and outstretched arm, and I give it to whomever I deem proper.   —Jeremiah 27:5

> Remember what happened a long time ago. For **Anochi-I, Source** Am God, and there is none other [in the office of] *Elohim;* there is none like Me.   —Isaiah 46:9

When the people transgress, it is **Anochi, I-Source**, who calls them to account.

> Hear, O Earth! **Anochi, I-Source** Am going to bring disaster upon this people, the outcome of their own schemes. For they would not hearken to My words, and they rejected My instruction.   —Jeremiah 6:19

Do you not consider this House, which bears My Name to be a den of thieves? As for Me, **Anochi, I-Source** have been watching [through My representative] YHWH. —JEREMIAH 7:11

And now say to the men of Judah and the inhabitants of Jerusalem: "Thus says YHWH: '**Anochi, I-Source** Am devising disaster for you and laying plans against you. Turn back, each of you, from your wicked ways, and mend your ways and actions.'" —JEREMIAH 18:11

If **Anochi, I-Source** Am bringing punishment upon the city that bears My Name, do you expect to go unpunished? You will not go unpunished, for I Am summoning the sword against all the inhabitants of the Earth, declares YHWH of the Array. —JEREMIAH 25:29

Pay heed, My people, and I will speak. I will bear witness against you. I Am **Anochi, I-Source.** —PSALMS 50:7

Yet, **Anochi** always holds out the possibility of repentance, and hope, and promise of redemption and return.

. . . Perhaps they will listen and turn back, each from his evil way, that I may renounce the punishment that **Anochi, I-Source** Am planning to bring upon them for their wicked acts. —JEREMIAH 26:3

For **Anochi, I-Source** Am mindful of the plans I have made concerning you—declares YHWH—plans for your welfare, not for disaster, to give you a hopeful future. —JEREMIAH 29:11

Can a woman forget her baby, or disown the child of her womb? Though she might forget, **Anochi, I-Source** could never forget you. —ISAIAH 49:15

To emphasize the unequivocal promise of redemption, **Anochi** speaks in **Anochi** voice not once, but twice in a number of prophetic verses.

It is **Anochi, I-Source, Anochi, I-Source** who—for My own sake—wipe away your transgressions, and remember your sins no more. —ISAIAH 43:25

So says YHWH: "Captives shall be taken from a warrior. And spoil shall be retrieved from a tyrant. For, **Anochi, I-Source** shall contend with your adversaries, and **Anochi, I-Source** will deliver your children." —ISAIAH 49:25

So says YHWH: "As I have brought this terrible disaster upon this people, so **Anochi, I-Source** Am going to bring upon them vast good fortune, which **Anochi, I-Source** have promised them." —JEREMIAH 32:42

And she shall gain through Me renown, joy, fame, and glory, and above all, the nations of the Earth, when they hear all the good fortune that **Anochi, I-Source** provide for them, they will thrill and quiver because of all the good fortune and prosperity that **Anochi, I-Source** provide for her. —JEREMIAH 33:9

Anochi, I-Source, Anochi, I-Source [through my representative] YHWH: None but I can triumph. —ISAIAH 43:11

Anochi, I-Source, Anochi, I-Source Am the One who comforts you. . . . —ISAIAH 51:12

And, **Anochi** fulfills the promise of redemption and return from both physical and spiritual exile.

Then you shall dwell in the land which I gave to your ancestors, and you shall be My people, and **Anochi, I-Source** will be [in the office of] your *Elohim*. —EZEKIEL 36:28

In case there is any question about the fullness of Source, and **Anochi, I-Source's** role in the history and life of the people, **Anochi, I-Source** makes it very clear, in the book of Psalms, the soul-cries of a people and their God.

In their times of greatest joy and fulfillment, it is **Anochi, I-Source** who encourages, and champions, and rejoices with the people. At their times of shatteredness and brokenness, at the times of the darkest nights of their souls, it is **Anochi, I-Source** who reassures, comforts, and shines the light of hope and redemption for the people.

I Am Anochi, I-Source [who placed] YHWH [in the office of] *Elohim*, who brought you out of the land of Egypt; open your mouth wide and I will fill it.   —PSALMS 81:11

Because he is devoted to me, I will deliver him; I will keep him safe, because he knows My Name. When he calls on Me, I will answer him; **Anochi, I-Source** will be with him in his distress. I will rescue him and honor him.   —PSALMS 91:15

THE HUMAN VOICE

When Joshua—who is a worthy successor of Moses and a loyal servant to God and the Jewish people—reviews his life and charges his people before he dies, he reaches deeply into and reflects his own **Anochi-I, God Within**.

Now YHWH preserved me as He promised. It is forty-five years since YHWH made this promise to Moses, when Israel was journeying through the desert. And here **Anochi-I** Am today, eighty-five years old.   —JOSHUA 14:10

Anochi-I Am now going the way of all the Earth. Acknowledge with all your heart and soul that not one of the good things that YHWH [who is in the office] *Elohim* promised you has failed to happen; they have all come true for you; not a single one has failed.
                                   —JOSHUA 23:14

From the time the Israelites entered the Promised Land until the establishment of the monarchy (a period of approximately two hundred years, 1200 BCE–1000 BCE) tribes in the land were ruled by a loose confederation of political/spiritual leaders who became known as Judges.

One of the most famous of these Judges was Deborah—not only because she was a woman leader in an era dominated by men, but because she had finely honed leadership skills.

In the opening lines of what has come to be known as *Shirat Devorah*—"Deborah's Song," she acknowledges the source of her abilities and power, in a verse that speaks **Anochi-I, God Within**, not once but twice.

> Hear, O kings! Give ear, O potentates. **Anochi-I** will sing to YHWH. **Anochi-I** will sing to YHWH, [the One who is in the office of] *Elohim* of Israel. —JUDGES 5:3

In Judges, there is ample evidence that allegiance to and worship of the One God had not taken very strong hold in the land. Some would describe it as "religious chaos." A man named Micah (not to be confused with the later biblical prophet, Micah) makes a molten image—in clear violation of the commandment against making images of God—and sets it up in his house, proving that, "In those days, there was no king of Israel, and every man did as he pleased" (Judges 17:6).

A traveler passes by Micah's home, and Micah asks him the typical questions one asks a traveler. He responds,

> **Anochi-I** Am a Levite from Bethlehem of Judah, and **Anochi-I** Am traveling to take up residence wherever I can find a place. —JUDGES 17:9

Micah replies:

> Stay with me. . . and be a father and a priest to me, and **Anochi-I** will pay you ten shekels of silver a year, and an allowance for clothing and your food . . . —JUDGES 17:10

The theme of the "travel texts" of Genesis is echoed here. The travel is sourced by **Anochi**, and the traveler feels **Anochi Within**.

Even though Micah had built an idol, he must have sensed the traveler's God-energy, for he responds from his own **Anochi-Within**.

Although it is not good that religious chaos reigned, or that Micah had built an idol, or that the traveler agrees to be a priest in a household that has an idolatrous image, perhaps this is another dramatic example of "**Anochi** was in this place, and I was not aware." Perhaps it is an opening to the sense of **Anochi** that is to come.

In the oft-echoed biblical motif of the barren wife, Elkanah has two wives. Peninnah has many children; Hannah (most likely the favorite wife) is barren. Each year, when they all go to make sacrificial worship to God at Shiloh, Peninnah taunts Hannah for being childless, and, in her sad misery, Hannah weeps.

Hannah's husband asks if his own GodSelf is not enough for her:

> Her husband Elkanah said to her, "Hannah, why are you crying, and why are you not eating? Why are you so sad? Am **Anochi-I** not more devoted to you than ten sons?"   —I SAMUEL 1:8

Hannah prays and prays for a child. When she is in the midst of her ecstatic prayer, the priest Eli thinks that she is intoxicated.

> Oh, no, my lord! My **Anochi-I**, **God Within**, is very unhappy. I have drunk no wine or other strong drink, but I have been pouring out my heart to YHWH.   —I SAMUEL 1:15

Hannah vows that if she gives birth to a son, he will be dedicated to serving God. Her prayers are answered; she births Samuel. After three years he is weaned, and she brings him to serve God at Shiloh. And indeed, Samuel will become one of the great seers and Judges of the Jewish nation, and will, eventually, be instrumental in establishing the monarchy. Thus, the barren wife brings her greatest GodSelf, her **Anochi-I**, **God Within** to fulfill her prayer and vow, and provides a great leader to the Jewish people.

When she brings her beloved son to Eli the priest, to dedicate him to holy work, her GodSelf, **God Within**, says,

> **Anochi-I** lend him to YHWH; for as long as he lives, he is lent to YHWH. . . .   —I SAMUEL 1:28

To be a prophet, a person has to not only hear or see the word of God, but also must be in full and confident touch with **Anochi-I**, **God Within**.

The prophet Isaiah describes:

> Here **Anochi-I** stand, (along with) the children whom YHWH has given me, as signs and portents in Israel. . . .   —ISAIAH 8:18

Isaiah serves **Anochi** by acting from his **Anochi-I, God Within**.

> And like a lion he called out, "On my Master's [Lord's] look-out, **Anochi-I** stand always by day, and at my post, I watch every night."   —ISAIAH 21:8

Jeremiah, too, echoes the call of **Anochi** coming through his **Anochi Within**.

> But just listen to this word which **Anochi-I** address to you and to all the people.   —JEREMIAH 28:7

Much like all prophets, Amos was spurned and rejected for his blunt, accusatory prophecies. (A question on a rabbinical school final examination asked, "Would you like Amos, or Isaiah, or Jeremiah to be your next door neighbor?")

Being a prophet was not much fun, but it was a calling, and when **Anochi** calls, the prophet—reluctant and modest as he was—responds and fulfills his mission.

The only way to succeed as a prophet—to not run away or go mad—was to burn away all ego, accept the assignment, and speak as a mouthpiece of **Anochi** from the depths of **Anochi-I, God Within**—even if, as in the case of Amos, he never saw himself that way.

> Amos answered, . . . "**Anochi-I** Am not a prophet, and **Anochi-I** Am not the son of a prophet. **Anochi-I** Am a cattle breeder and a tender of sycamore trees."   —AMOS 7:14

One of the most poignant books of the Bible—and surely the one that has served humanity throughout the millennia as a paradigmatic debate about the issue of good and evil—is the book of Job.

To test his faith, God takes away everything from Job—his children, all his wealth, and material possessions. At first, Job accepts the decree against him, but at a certain point, he rails against God. Job's friends come and urge him to renounce God. Ultimately, Job's faith is strong. He often speaks from his **Anochi-I, God Within**.

How then can **Anochi-I** answer [God]? Or choose my arguments against [God]?   —JOB 9:14

It is **Anochi-I** who Am in the wrong. Why should I waste the effort?   —JOB 9:29

But I, like you, have a mind, and **Anochi-I** Am not less than you. . . .
                                    —JOB 12:3

Job counters:

Anochi-I would also like to talk to you if you were in my place. I would barrage you with words. I would wag my head over you.
                                    —JOB 16:4

After listening to all the criticism against his unwavering faith, Job says:

Bear with me when **Anochi-I** speak, and after I have spoken, you can mock. Is the complaint of my **Anochi-I** directed against man? Why should I not lose my patience [with you, my friend]? —JOB 21:3

Job contends that there is nothing that he has done that has brought this fate upon him. In modern words, he would say, "Life happens." And this, to Job, is part of the natural order, and no reason to lose faith in God.

I am guiltless, free from transgression. **Anochi-I** Am innocent, without iniquity.   —JOB 33:9

God finally appears and, from out of a whirlwind, permits Job to see the wonders of the world. Job understands; he acknowledges his place in the vast universe of God's plan. He says to God:

Indeed, I spoke without understanding of the things which are beyond me that I did not know.   —JOB 42:3

Hear now, and **Anochi-I** will speak; I will ask and You will inform me. I had heard You with my ears, but now I see You with my eyes. Therefore, I recant and relent, being but dust and ashes. —Job 42: 4–5

The end of the story comes when Job celebrates his **Anochi-I, God Within** GodSelf, and affirms his understanding of **Anochi's** design in **Anochi's** world.

One of world literature's greatest books of soul-cries of both pain and joy to God is the biblical book of Psalms. Here the psalmist calls out to God from the depths of **Anochi-I, God Within**:

> Hear my prayer, O, YHWH. Give ear to my cry; do not disregard my tears. For, like my forebears, **Anochi-I**, Am a stranger to You.
> —Psalms 39:13

> May my prayer be pleasing [to God] **Anochi-I** rejoice in YHWH.
> —Psalms 104:34

> **Anochi-I** Am only a sojourner in the land; do not hide Your commandments from me.　　　　　—Psalms 119:19

> Though I am belittled and despised, **Anochi-I** have not neglected Your precepts.　　　　　—Psalms 119:141

> **Anochi-I** rejoice over Your promise. . . .　　　　—Psalms 119:162

IN DIALOGUE

In Prophets and Writings, there are powerful dialogues between **Anochi, I-Source** and prophets who are deeply in touch with their **Anochi-I, God Within**.

The call to prophecy is resisted by Jeremiah, because he does not think that his **Anochi-I, God Within** is well enough developed. When God designates Jeremiah, the soon-to-be prophet replies,

> Ah! YHWH, God: I do not know how to speak, because **Anochi-I, God Within**, Am still a boy.　　　　—Jeremiah 1:6

God rejects the argument.

Do not say, "**Anochi-I, God Within,** Am still a boy." But, go wherever I send you, and speak whatever I command.   —JEREMIAH 1:7

You, Jeremiah, are a prophet. **Anochi** says so. "So, you, gird up your loins. Arise and speak to them all that **Anochi, I-Source** command you. . . .   —JEREMIAH 1:17

One of the most well-known of all biblical stories is of the prophet Jonah. God tells Jonah to go to the town of Nineveh, and tell the people that, because of their sins, they and their city will be destroyed.

Jonah does not want the assignment, and flees. He boards a boat to sail away, but a great storm arises, and the sailors surmise that the storm is the fault of one of them. They cast lots, and the lot falls on Jonah.

Tell us, the sailors ask, why has this misfortune come upon us? Who are you? From where do you come; what are your origins?

With no hesitation, Jonah replies, touching his GodSelf:

Anochi-I Am a Hebrew. I worship YHWH [in the office of] *Elohim,* the God in Heaven, who made both sea and land.   —JONAH 1:9

It is not long before Jonah realizes that he cannot flee from nor hide from God. For, when it comes to this major assignment, God calls upon the fullness of Source to give the charge.

The word of YHWH came to Jonah a second time. Go at once to Nineveh, that great city, and proclaim what **Anochi, I-Source** tell you.   —JONAH 3:1–2

These texts assuredly establish: As in Torah, the appearance of **Anochi** in Prophets and Writings clearly and always indicates the presence of **Anochi, I-Source**, the whole, complete God, or of **Anochi-I, God Within**.

APPENDIX II

A LISTING OF ALL
ANOCHI BIBLICAL TEXTS

THE VERY BEST way to meet and know **Anochi, I-Source**, and to touch **Ancohi-I** is to read and study the biblical texts where **Anochi** appears.

You can deepen your relationship with **Anochi**, and experience **Anochi's** continuing revelation by studying the **Anochi** texts on your own, or better, by joining with friends to form an **Anochi** Study Group.

From the pages of antiquity, **Anochi** will speak, and we will all come to listen. More will be given; more will be revealed.

This book contains prime examples of the use of **Anochi, I-Source**, and **Anochi-I** in the Bible.

Here, in order, are the source-text citations of **all** the appearances of the word **Anochi** in the Bible—141 appearances of the word **Anochi** in 135 verses in the Torah; and 218 appearances in 200 verses within the second and third sections of the Hebrew Bible, Prophets and Writings.

The verses that are quoted in this book are indicated with an asterisk (*).

TORAH

Genesis

3:10*
4:9*
7:4
15:1
15:2
15:14*
16:5*
16:8
18:27*
19:19
20:6
21:24
21:26
23:4*
24:3*
24:13*
24:24*
24:27*
24:31*
24:34
24:37
24:42
24:43
25:22*
24:30*
25:32*
26:24
27:11
27:19*
28:15*
28:16*
28:20*
29:33
30:1*
30:2*

30:3
30:30*
31:1*
31:5*
31:38*
31:39*
32:12*
37:16*
38:17
38:25
43:9
46:3*
46:4*
47:30*
48:21
50:5
50:21
50:24

Exodus

3:6*
3:11*
3:12
3:13
4:10*
4:11*
4:12*
4:15*
4:23
7:17*
7:27
8:24*
8:25*
17:9
19:9*
20:2*

20:5*
23:20*
32:18
34:10
34:11*

Numbers

4:8
11:12
11:14*
11:21
22:30*
22:32*
23:15*

Deuteronomy

4:1*
4:2*
4:22
4:40
5:1
5:5
5:6
5:9
5:31
6:2
6:6*
7:11
8:1
8:11
10:10
10:13
11:8
11:13
11:22
11:26*

11:27
11:28
11:32
12:11
12:14
12:28
13:1
13:19
15:5
15:11
15:15
18:19
19:7
19:9
24:18
24:22
27:1
27:4
27:10
28:1
28:13
28:14
28:15
29:13
30:2
30:8
30:11
30:16
31:2*
31:18*
31:23*
31:27
32:40
32:46*

PROPHETS

Joshua
1:2*
7:20
11:6
13:6
14:7
14:8
14:10*
23:14*
24:15

Judges
5:3*
6:8
6:15
6:18
6:37
7:17
7:18
8:5
11:9
11:27
11:35
11:37
17:9*
17:10*
19:18

I Samuel
1:8*
1:15*
1:28*
2:23
2:24
3:11

3:39
4:16
7:2
9:19
9:21
10:8
10:18
12:23
15:14
16:3
17:8
17:43
17:45
18:18
18:23
20:5
20:36
21:3
22:22
23:17
24:5
30:13

II Samuel
1:8
1:16
2:6
2:20
3:8
3:13
3:28
7:18
11:5
12:7*
13:28

14:18
15:28
18:12
19:36
20:17
20:19

I Kings
2:2
2:16
2:18
2:20
3:7
4:13
14:6
19:4
22:19

Isaiah
6:5
8:18*
21:8*
43:11*
43:12
43:25*
44:24*
45:12
45:13
46:9*
49:15*
49:25*
50:5
51:12
51:15
54:11

54:16
66:13
66:18
11:14
14:12
18:11*
23:32
24:7
25:15
25:16
25:27
25:29*
26:3*
26:5
27:5*
27:6
28:7*
29:11*
29:23
30:22*
31:32
32:42*
33:9*
34:13
35:14
36:3
50:9
51:64

Jeremiah
1:6*
1:7*
1:17*
2:21
3:14

3:19	*Micah*	9:35
4:6	3:8	12:3*
6:19*		13:2
7:11*	*Zechariah*	13:22
	11:6	14:15
Ezekiel	11:16	16:4*
36:2*	12:2	21:3*
		21:4*
Hosea	*Malachai*	29:16
1:9	3:23*	33:9*
2:4		33:31
2:10	**WRITINGS**	42:4*
2:16	*Psalms*	*Ruth*
5:14	22:7	
7:13	39:13*	2:10
11:3	46:11*	2:13
11:9	50:7*	3:9
12:10	75:4	3:12
12:11	81:11*	3:13
13:4	91:15*	4:4
	104:34*	
Amos	109:22	*Daniel*
2:9	119:19*	10:11
2:10	119:141*	
2:13	119:162*	*Nehemiah*
4:7	141:10	1:6
5:1		
6:8	*Proverbs*	*I Chronicles*
7:14*	24:32*	17:1
9:9	30:2	
Jonah	*Job*	
1:9*	9:2*	
3:2*	9:14*	

In every place where I cause My Name to be
mentioned,
I will come to you and bless you.

—Exodus 20:21

NOTES

Some of the poems, prayers, and meditations are written by the author and/or his wife.

They are cited in the text as WD for Wayne Dosick, and ELKD for Ellen Linda Kaufman Dosick.

PRELUDE. BORN TO LOVE

1. After Hosea 2:21.
2. Adaptation of Jeremiah 1:5.

CHAPTER 1. HERE ON EARTH

1. William Wordsworth, "Ode to Intimations of Immortality."
2. Paraphrasing Rabbi Seymour Prystowsky, "Come Let Us Reason Together," a sermon delivered at National Association of Retired Reform Rabbis Convention, January 8, 2011.
3. Robert Bly, "What Stories Do We Need?" Recorded lecture by the author. Better!Listen.com. Digital download.
4. Phrase (also "the death of God") made popular by the theologian Dr. Richard L. Rubenstein in his book, *After Auschwitz,* Indianapolis, New York: The Bobbs-Merrill Co., 1966, in describing God after the Holocaust; and by the *TIME* magazine cover and cover story, "Is God Dead?" John T. Elson, ed., April 8, 1966.
5. A. N. Brown, private conversation.
6. I Kings 19:12.
7. Genesis 32:3; Exodus 33:11; Exodus 33:20–23; Deuteronomy 5:4; Deuteronomy 34:10; Judges 6:22; Ezekiel 20:35.
8. Rabbi Shlomo Carlebach *zt"l* (1925–1994) recording of *Hu Elokeinu* on the audio tape, *U'vene Yerushalayim.*

CHAPTER 2. THE NAMES OF GOD

1. *An explanation of why the name YHWH is used throughout the book of Genesis.*

   Whether we accept the traditional view that the Torah was written down by Moses, transcribing the exact word of God, or whether we accept the view of modern scholarship that it was written by many Divinely inspired authors over a long period of time, and redacted by an editor, one thing is certain: The Torah was written long after the early Genesis events it describes.

   By the time the Torah was set in writing, there were many oral traditions about God and the ancient Hebrews. These stories wove together myths from antiquity with ongoing tribal legends and contemporaneous experience. Many of the names of God were known and often used interchangeably. Each had achieved a level of sanctity through its usage and telling. By the time the text was recorded, the Hebrews were forged into a "nation" or, at least, a cohesive "people," through the exodus from Egypt, the revelation at Sinai, and the entrance into the Promised Land of Israel. Many of the earlier names for God faded from center-consciousness. The predominant God-name of the time—YHWH (Adonai)—took precedence, and was superimposed by the Torah writer(s) onto many of the earlier stories.

2. Joel T. Klein, *Through the Name of God: A New Road to the Origin of Judaism and Christianity* (Westport, Conn., Greenwood Press, 2001).

3. Mark Sameth, "Who Is He? He Is She: The Secret Four-Letter Name of God," *The Reform Jewish Quarterly* (New York: Central Conference of American Rabbis, Summer 2008).

4. *A continuing discussion of the many names of God.*

   As if all these names for God were not enough: The Talmud (Babylonian Talmud, Kiddushin 71a) refers to a twelve-letter Name of God, which has been lost to us. Some say that this twelve-letter Name was derived from the *Bircat HaCohanim,* the Priestly Blessing (Numbers 6:24–26). There is also a little-known tradition of a 14-letter name of God, taken from a verse of Torah, which has become the central prayer of the Jewish worship service *S'hma Yisrael* (Deuteronomy 6:4). The concept of a lost 42-letter Name of God is revived and reflected in a second-century prayer, *Ana B'Ko-ach.* The idea of a 72-letter Name of God comes from a complex combination of letters in verses 19–21 in the fourteenth chapter of the biblical Book of Exodus. One tradition teaches that this 72-letter Name was inscribed on the breastplate of the High Priest, and was consulted by the Priest as a type of oracle (Babylonian Talmud, *Yoma* 73b). This 72-letter Name has received notoriety in recent days, popularized by contemporary Kabbalists. There are also traditions of a 22-letter Name of God, and a 33-letter Name of God. We get the message: throughout history, Torah scholars have known that the real Name of God has been missing, and have been speculating about it and searching for it for a long time!

5. *An explanation of the Yom Kippur ritual invoking the name of God.*

The mystical tradition explains: (Zohar *Bamidbar*, 146b–147a) "The Divine Name has both a revealed and an undisclosed form. In its revealed form, it is written YHWH, but in its undisclosed form, it is written in other letters. . . . Even the revealed form of the Name [YHWH] is hidden under other letters. . . . It behooves the High Priest to concentrate on the various permutations of the Divine Name. . . . In these letters of this Name are concealed all twenty-two attributes of [God's] mercy . . . but they combine in one composite Name, on which the High Priest concentrates his mind. At the time when the Name was disclosed, the Priest would concentrate his mind on its deep and inner meaning, and would utter the Name in such as way as to be in accord with that meaning."

This yearly entrance into the Holy of Holies to speak the Name of God was such a powerful and dramatic moment in the life of the people, that it is re-enacted in the liturgy of the Yom Kippur worship service, even to this day.

The account, originally sourced in the second century *Mishnah*, is described in English translation in contemporary prayer books:

> The Priests [that is all the Priests except the High Priest] and the people were standing in the Courtyard when they heard the *Shem HaM'fo'rash*, the glorious and awesome Ineffable [some translate as "Explicit," or "Explained," or "Ultimate"] Name of God coming from the mouth of the High Priest, in holiness and purity, and they would kneel, and prostrate themselves, and fall on their faces, and say: "Blessed is the Name of God, in glorious Sovereignty, forever and *ever.*"
>
> *(Translation of this Yom Kippur ritual adapted from various sources by the author.)*
>
> With the destruction of the second Holy Temple and the exile of the people in 70 CE, this Yom Kippur ritual was lost, and, with it, the transmitted knowledge of the proper pronunciation of the Name of God—or, more likely, the real Name of God that was the hidden secret of the High Priest.

6. Known as the Documentary Hypothesis, offered by Julius Wellhausen in *Prolegomena*, preceded by the work of Karl Heinrich Graf and Wilhelm Vatke, based on the earlier work of Witter, Astruc, and Eichhorn.

CHAPTER 3. GOD—FOUND!

1. For a complete discussion of the *Anunnaki,* see Zecharia Sitchin, *The 12th Planet: Book I of the Earth Chronicles* (Rochester, Vt.: Bear & Co., 1991); Alan F. Alford, *Gods of the New Millennium: Scientific Proof of Flesh and Blood Gods* (Walsall, England: Eridu Books, 1966), and Alan F. Alford, *When the Gods Came Down: The Catastrophic Roots of Religion Revealed* (London: Hodder & Stoughton, 2000).

2. *Further evidence that the sages knew that* **Anochi** *is the real Name of God.*

    In the Talmud (Babylonian Talmud, *Shabbat* 105a), Rabbi Yochanan teaches that **Anochi** is an acronym for the words, *Ana Nafshi Ketivat Yehavit,* "I Myself wrote (and) gave the Torah." Other sages give different interpretations of the acronym, all focused on their understanding that the "I-ness" of Source is inherent in the word **Anochi.** But the time was not energetically right for them to reveal what they knew.

    Similarly, knowing that the name of God is nowhere in the biblical book of Esther, the sages (Babylonian Talmud, *Chulin* 139b) ask: "Where in the Torah is there an allusion to the story of Queen Esther?" In a complex word-play involving the Hebrew name of Esther, Rav Masnah, quoting Deuteronomy 31:18, answers: *"V'Anochi hastir astir,"* "I will surely conceal [My countenance from them]." The sage teaches: The real Name of God is not only absent from the book of Esther, but it (and God) is hiding from the people.

    The Chasidic Rabbi, Mordechai Yosef Leiner of Isbitza, known as the Isbitzer Rebbe (1801–1854), explains: [When God gave the Ten Commandments] the word *Ani* is not used for "I," but, rather, **Anochi.** Had it been written *Ani,* the meaning would have been that the Holy One had revealed His Light to Israel in all its completeness. . . . However, the additional letter [*kaf*] in [the word] **Anochi** teaches that it is not a state of completeness, yet, rather, an imagined image of the Light that the Holy One would reveal in the future." (*Yitro,* selection 1, "I Am")

INTERLUDE. SEEK AND YE SHALL FIND

1. Menachem Mendel of Kotzk, the Kotzker Rebbe (1787–1859).

CHAPTER 6. **ANOCHI** AND US

1. Laurence Cossé, *A Corner of the Veil* (New York: Scribner, 1996).

2. Wayne Dosick and Ellen Kaufman Dosick, *20-Minute Kabbalah: The Daily Personal Spiritual Practice That Brings You to God, Your Soul-Knowing, and Your Heart's Desires* (Cardiff-by-the-Sea, Calif.: Waterside Publishing, 2007).

INTERLUDE. THE FACE IN
THE MIRROR IS YOUR OWN

1. Alternately attributed to Ralph Waldo Emerson (1803–1882) and Oliver Wendell Holmes (1841–1935) http://quoteinvestigator.com/2011/01/11/what-lies-within.

CHAPTER 7. ANOCHI WITHIN

1. Rabbi David A. Cooper, *God Is a Verb: Kabbalah and the Practice of Mystical Judaism* (New York: Riverhead Books, 1997).
2. Walt Whitman (1819–1892), "We Two, How Long We Were Fool'd," *Leaves of Grass*.
3. Chaim Potok *zt"l* (1925–2002), *The Gift of Asher Lev* (New York: Farrar, Fawcett Crest, 1990).
4. Abraham Joshua Heschel *zt"l* (1907–1972), *Man Is Not Alone* (New York: Farrar, Straus, Giroux, 1976).
5. Rabbi David Wolfe Blank *zt"l* (1950–1998).
6. Rabbi Burt Jacobson.
7. President Abraham Lincoln, quoted by many in public life. There is no record of this exact statement; it seems to summarize a number of sentiments expressed by Lincoln on the subject of God and prayer.
8. Abraham Joshua Heschel *zt"l*, "On Prayer," *Conservative Judaism* 25, 1, Fall 1970.
9. The Lord's Prayer, Matthew 6:13, and known in a number of variant versions.
10. *"feed the hungry"*—after Leviticus 19:19; *"care for the widow . . ."* Exodus 22:21; *"tell the truth"* Exodus 23:1; *"give fair weights . . ."* Leviticus 19:35; *"pay the laborer . . ."* Leviticus 19:13; *"honor parents"* Exodus 20:12; *"be kind to the stranger"* Exodus 22:20; and Deuteronomy 10:19; *"do not put a stumbling block before the blind"* Leviticus 19:14; *"love your neighbor . . ."* Leviticus 19:18.
11. Alan Paton (1903–1998), *The United Methodist Hymnal* #456, quoted in *Peacemaking Day by Day*, v. 2 (Washington D.C.: Pax Christi USA, 1989).
12. Rabbi Jules Harlow, in *Mahzor for Rosh Hashanah and Yom Kippur* (New York: The Rabbinical Assembly, 1972).
13. Laurence Cossé, *A Corner of the Veil* (New York: Scribner, 1996).
14. Elie Wiesel, quoted by Alice L. Eckardt, "Rebel against God," *Face to Face*, 6, 1979.
15. Aaron Zeitlin *zt"l* (1898–1973), "If You Look at the Stars and Yawn," translated by Emanuel Goldsmith.
16. Exodus 34:30.

17. Babylonian Talmud, *Menachot* 43a. Rabbi Max Kudishin *zt"l* termed this practice "normal mysticism."

18. First Epistle to the Thessalonians 5:17.

19. *Rabbi Nachman's Wisdom*, Breslov Research Institute, quoted in *The Empty Chair: Finding Hope and Joy* (Woodstock, Vt: Jewish Lights Publishing, 1994).

20. Aldous Huxley (1894–1963).

21. From adaption of Hebrew prayer, *Sabbath and Festival Prayerbook,* edited by Morris Silverman (New York: The Rabbinical Assembly and the United Synagogue of America, 1946).

22. Rabbi Danya Ruttenberg, *Surprised by God: How I Learned to Stop Worrying and Love Religion* (Boston: Beacon Press, 2008).

23. Rabbi Levi Yitzchak of Berditchev *zt"l* (1740–1809), translated by Rabbi Burt Jacobson, adapted by Wayne Dosick.

24. Based on rabbinic interpretation of "Whatever happens, it was designated long ago, and it was known that it would happen." (Ecclesiastes 6:10) and the legend of all souls being present at Mt. Sinai to receive the Commandments. For a full explanation, see Schwartz, *Tree of Souls: The Mythology of Judaism* Oxford: Oxford University Press, 2004).

    The explanation of life and death and the eternity of the soul is the teaching of Wayne Dosick.

25. Theodore Roethke (1908-1963), "Infirmity."

26. A variation of *Shaddai Tamid,* from the morning prayer *El Baruch.*

27. Wayne Dosick.

INTERLUDE. WHO KNOWS ONE?

1. Abraham Joshua Heschel *zt"l.*

CHAPTER 8. **ANOCHI'S** PROMISE

1. This comes from my childhood in Chicago, when we would play Hopscotch. The top box—the goal of the game—was not called "10," "Goal," or "Home," as it was in most places, but "Sky Blue," which became my image of the place of ultimate perfection.

2. Wayne Dosick.

3. Judy Chicago, "Merger," popularly known as "Eden Once Again."

CHAPTER 9. THE AFFIRMATION

1. Adaptation of verse recited following *Sh'ma Yisrael* in the Jewish worship service; based on Psalms 72:19; and on the response of the worshippers in

the Courtyard of the Holy Temple, to hearing the Name of God recited by the High Priest in the Holy of Holies on Yom Kippur.

POSTLUDE: **ANOCHI, ANOCHI**

1. "Return us . . ." Lamentations 5:21 and Holy Ark prayer: *Etz Chaim*; *". . . as at the very, very Beginning"* Rabbi Jack Riemer; *"struts and frets . . ."*; William Shakespeare, *Macbeth,* V, V; "Blessed Am I . . ." variation of "Blessed are we . . ." Deuteronomy 28:6.

EPILOGUE: A PERSONAL WORD

1. Rabbi Shmuel Smelke of Nikolsburg *zt"l* (1726–1778).
2. Moses Maimonides *zt"l* (1135–1204).
3. Martin Buber *zt"l* (1878–1965) from "Religion as Presence" lecture course, January–March 1922, translated and presented by Rivka Horowitz, *Buber's Way to "I and Thou": The Development of Martin Buber's Thought and His "Religion as Presence Lectures"* (Philadelphia: Jewish Publication Society, 1998).
4. Isaiah 6:8; Genesis 26:24; and thirteen additional citations in *Tanakh.*
5. Sir James Hopwood Jeans (1877–1946), British physicist and astronomer, "The New World—Picture of Modern Physics," in *Science 7,* September 1934.
6. POGO, cartoon character created by syndicated cartoonist Walt Kelly (1913–1973).
7. Carl Gustav Jung (1875–1961), from the full quote "Bidden or unbidden, God is present." Jung discovered the original statement, *"Vocatus atoue non vocatus Deus adverit"*—"Called or uncalled, God is present" in the Latin writings of the Dutch scholar Desiderius Erasmus (1466–1536), who quoted it from a Spartan proverb. Jung slightly changed the wording, and popularized it by having it inscribed on the doorway of his house and on his gravestone.
8. Rabbi Lawrence Kushner, *Invisible Lines of Connections: Sacred Stories from the Ordinary* (Woodstock, Vt.: Jewish Lights Publishing, 1996).
9. Eliphas Levi (1810–1875).
10. Clarence Kaufman *zt"l* (1922–2007) and Wayne Dosick.

BIBLIOGRAPHY

Biblical quotations are taken from *Tanakh, The Holy Scriptures: A New Translation According to the Traditional Hebrew Text*, Philadelphia: Jewish Publication Society, 1985, or from the author's own translation.

Translations of the **Anochi** texts are the author's.

Translations of The Soncino Talmud, The Soncino Zohar, and The Soncino Midrash on the Soncino Classics CD-ROM have been adapted by the author.

All biblical and classical Rabbinic literature source references are noted in the running text of the book.

Alford, Alan F. *Gods of the New Millennium: Scientific Proof of Flesh and Blood Gods*. Walsall, England: Eridu Books, 1996.

———. *When the Gods Came Down: The Catastrophic Roots of Religion Revealed*. London, England: Hodder & Stoughton, 2000.

Alter, Robert. *The Five Books of Moses: A Translation with Commentary*. New York: W.W. Norton & Company, 2004.

Armstrong, Karen. *The Battle for God: A History of Fundamentalism*. New York: The Random House Publishing Group, 2000.

———. *A History of God: The 4,000 Year Quest of Judaism, Christianity and Islam*. New York: Alfred A. Knopf, 1994.

———. *The Bible: A Biography*. New York: Atlantic Monthly Press, 2007.

———. *The Case for God*. New York: Alfred A. Knopf, 2009.

———. *The Great Transformation: The Beginning of Our Religious Traditions*. New York: Anchor Books, 2006.

Benner, Jeff A. *His Name Is One: An Ancient Hebrew Perspective of the Names of God*. College Station, Tex.: Virtualbookworm.com Publishing, 2003.

Berlin, Adele, and Marc Zvi Brettler. Edited by Michael Fishbane. *The Jewish Study Bible: Featuring the Jewish Publication Society Tanakh Translation*. Oxford, New York: Oxford University Press, Inc., 2004.

Bloom, Harold. *Jesus and Yahweh: The Divine Names*. New York: Riverhead Books, 2005.

Bly, Robert. *What Stories Do We Need?* Recorded lecture by the author. Better!Listen.com. Digital download.

Bonaventura. *The Mind's Road to God*. Translated by George Boas. Saddle River, N.J.: Prentice Hall Library of Liberal Arts, 1953.

Borowtiz, Eugene B. *A New Jewish Theology in the Making*. Philadelphia, Pa.: The Westminster Press, 1968.

———. *Renewing the Covenant: A Theology for the Postmodern Jew*. Philadelphia, Pa.: The Jewish Publication Society, 1991.

Braden, Gregg. *The God Code: The Secret of Our Past, the Promise of Our Future*. Carlsbad, Calif.: Hay House Inc., 2004.

Breslov Research Institute. *Rabbi Nachman's Wisdom*. Quoted in *The Empty Chair: Finding Hope and Joy*, Woodstock, Vt.: Jewish Lights Publishing, 1994.

Brettler, Marc Zvi. *How to Read the Bible*. Philadelphia: The Jewish Publication Society, 2005.

Bright, John. *A History of Israel*. Philadelphia: The Westminster Press, n.d.

Budge, E. A. Wallis. *From Fetish to God in Ancient Egypt*. New York: Dover Publications, 1988.

Chan, Francis, with Diane Yankowski. *Crazy Love: Overwhelmed by a Relentless God*. Colorado Springs, Colo.: David C. Cook, 2008.

Cooper, Rabbi David A. *God is a Verb: Kabbalah and the Practice of Mystical Judaism*. New York: Riverhead Books, 1997.

Copan, Paul. *Is God a Moral Monster?: Making Sense of the Old Testament God*. Grand Rapids, Mich.: Baker Books, 2011.

Cossé, Laurence. *A Corner of the Veil*. New York: Scribner, 1996.

Cross, Frank Moore. *Canaanite Myth and Hebrew Epic: Essays in the History of the Religion of Israel*. Cambridge, Mass.: Harvard University Press, 1973.

———. *From Epic to Canon: History and Literature in Ancient Israel*. Baltimore, Md. and London, England: The Johns Hopkins University Press, 1998.

Debray, Regis. *God: An Itinerary*. Translated by Jeffrey Mehlman. London, New York: Verso, 2004.

Dever, William G. *Did God Have a Wife? Archaeology and Folk Religion in Ancient Israel*. Grand Rapids, Mich.: William B. Eerdmans Publishing Company, 2005.

———. *What Did the Biblical Writers Know and When Did They Know It? What Archaeology Can Tell Us about the Reality of Ancient Israel*. Grand Rapids, Mich.: William B. Eerdmans Publishing Company, 2001.

Diamond, Jared. *Collapse: How Societies Choose to Fail or Succeed*. New York: Penguin, 2005.

———. *Guns, Germs, and Steel: The Fates of Human Societies.* New York: W.W. Norton & Company, 1997.

Dosick, Rabbi Wayne. *Living Judaism: The Complete Guide to Jewish Belief, Tradition & Practice.* New York: HarperSanFrancisco, 1995.

———. *Soul Judaism: Dancing with God into a New Era.* Woodstock, Vt.: Jewish Lights Publishing, 1999.

———. *When Life Hurts: A Book of Hope.* New York: HarperSanFrancisco, 1998.

Dosick, Rabbi Wayne, and Ellen Kaufman Dosick. *20-Minute Kabbalah: The Daily Personal Spiritual Practice That Brings You to God, Your Soul-Knowing, and Your Heart's Desires.* Cardiff-by-the-Sea, Calif.: Waterside Publishing, 2007.

Ehrman, Bart D. *God's Problem: How the Bible Fails to Answer Our Most Important Question—Why We Suffer.* New York: HarperOne, 2008.

Eliade, Mircea. *The Sacred and the Profane: The Nature of Religion.* New York: Harcourt Inc, 1957.

Elson, John T., ed. "Is God Dead?" *Time,* April 8, 1966.

Feiler, Bruce. *Abraham: A Journey to the Heart of Three Faiths.* New York: William Morrow, 2002.

———. *Walking the Bible: A Journey by Land through the Five Books of Moses.* New York; William Morrow, 2001.

———. *Where God Was Born: A Journey by Land to the Roots of Religion.* New York: William Morrow, 2005.

Friedman, Richard Elliot. *Who Wrote the Bible?* New York: Summit Books, 1987.

———. *The Bible with Sources Revealed: A New View into the Five Books of Moses.* New York: HarperSanFrancisco, 2003.

———. *The Hidden Face of God.* New York: HarperSanFrancisco, 1995.

Goldstein, Rebecca Newberger. *36 Arguments for the Existence of God: A Work of Fiction.* New York: Pantheon Books, 2010.

Grabbe, Lester L. *Ancient Israel: What Do We Know and How Do We Know It?* London, England: T & T Clark, 2007.

Greenberg, Moshe. *Biblical Prose Prayer: As a Window to the Popular Religion of Ancient Israel.* Berkeley and Los Angeles: University of California Press, 1983.

Grizone, Joseph F. *Trinity: A New Living Spirituality.* New York: Doubleday, 2002.

Harlow, Jules, ed. *Mahzor for Rosh Hashanah and Yom Kippur.* New York: The Rabbinical Assembly, 1972.

Harrison, R. K. *Old Testament Times.* Grand Rapids, Mich.: William B. Eerdmans Publishing Company, 1970.

Heidel, Alexander. *The Babylonian Genesis: The Story of Creation.* 2nd ed. Chicago: The University of Chicago Press, 1942.

Hemphill, Ken. *The Names of God.* Nashville, Tenn.: Broadman & Hollman Publishers, 2001.

Heschel, Abraham Joshua. *Man Is Not Alone.* New York: Farrar, Straus, Giroux, 1976.

———. "On Prayer." *Conservative Judaism* 25, 1, Fall 1970.

Hess, Richard S. *Israelite Religions: An Archaeological and Biblical Survey.* Grand Rapids, Mich.: Baker Academics, 2007.

Hieronimus, J. Zohara Meyerhoff. *Kabbalistic Teachings of the Female Prophets: The Seven Holy Women of Ancient Israel.* Rochester, Vt.: Inner Traditions, 2008.

Hitchens, Christopher. *God is Not Great: How Religions Poison Everything.* New York and Boston: Twelve Hatchette Book Group, 2007.

Hoffman, Joel M. *In the Beginning: A Short History of the Hebrew Language.* New York: New York University Press, 2004.

Horwitz, Rivka. *Buber's Way to "I and Thou": The Development of Martin Buber's Thought and His "Religion as Presence" Lectures.* Philadelphia: Jewish Publication Society, 1989.

Jacobs, A. J. *The Year of Living Biblically: One Man's Humble Quest to Follow the Bible as Literally as Possible.* New York: Simon & Schuster, 2007.

James, E. O. *The Ancient Gods.* Edison, N.J.: Castle Books, 2004.

Jeans, Sir James Hopwood. "The New World—Picture of Modern Physics." *Science 7,* September, 1934.

Jordan, Michael. *Encyclopedia of Gods: Over 25,000 Deities of the World.* New York: Facts on File, Inc., 1993.

Keller, Timothy. *The Reason for God: Belief in an Age of Skepticism.* New York: Dutton, 2008.

Klein, Joel T. *Through the Name of God: A New Road to the Origin of Judaism and Christianity.* Westport, Conn.; London: Greenwood Press, 2001.

Knohl, Israel. *The Divine Symphony: The Bible's Many Voices.* Philadelphia, Pa.: The Jewish Publication Society, 2003.

Kornberg, Rabbi Jamie S. *The God Upgrade: Finding Your 21st-Century Spirituality in Judaism's 5,000-Year-Old Tradition.* Woodstock, Vt.: Jewish Lights Publishing, 2011.

Kramer, Samuel Noah. *History Begins at Sumer.* New York: A Doubleday Anchor Book, 1959.

Kushner, Lawrence. *God Was in This Place and I, I Did Not Know.* Woodstock, Vt.: Jewish Lights Publishing, 1994.

Leeming, David, with Margaret Leeming. *A Dictionary of Creation Myths.* New York: Oxford University Press, 1994.

Lightfoot, Neil R. *How We Got the Bible.* New York: MJF Books, 2003.

Kugel, James L. *The Bible as It Was.* Cambridge, Mass.: The Belknapp Press of Harvard University, 1997.

———. *The God of Old: Inside the Lost World of the Bible.* New York: The Free Press, 2003.

Mazar, Amihai. *Archaeology of the Land of the Bible—10,000–586 BCE.* New York: Doubleday, 1990.

Micklethwait, John, and Adrian Wooldridge. *God is Back: How the Global Revival of Faith is Changing the World.* New York: Penguin Press, 2009.

Miles, Jack. *God: A Biography.* New York: Vintage Books, 1995.

Mulder, Martin Jan, ed., and Harry Sysling, exec. ed., *Mikra: Text, Translation, Reading and Interpretation of the Hebrew Bible in Ancient Judaism and Early Christianity.* Peabody, Mass.: Hendrickson Publisher, 2004.

Muffs, Dr. Yochanan. *The Personhood of God: Biblical Theology, Human Faith and the Divine Image.* Woodstock, Vt.: Jewish Lights Publishing, 2005.

Mykoff, Moshe, adapter. *The Empty Chair: Finding Hope and Joy: Timeless Wisdom from a Hasidic Master, Rebbe Nachman of Breslov.* Woodstock, Vt.: Jewish Lights Publishing, 1994.

Newberg, Andrew, MD; Eugene D'Aguili, MD, PhD.; and Vince Rause. *Why God Won't Go Away: Brain Science and the Biology of Belief.* New York: Ballantine Books, 2001.

Novak, Michael. *No One Sees God: The Dark Night of Atheists and Believers.* New York: Doubleday, 2008.

Novick, Rabbi Leah. *On the Wings of Shekhinah: Rediscovering Judaism's Divine Feminine.* Wheaton, Ill.: Quest Books; Theosophical Publishing House, 2008.

O'Brien, Joan, and Wilfred Major. *In the Beginning: Creation Myths from Ancient Mesopotamia, Israel and Greece.* n.p.: American Academy of Religion, Scholars Press, 1982.

Palmer, Michael. *The Question of God: An Introduction and Sourcebook.* London, New York: Routledge, 2001.

Paton, Alan. *The United Methodist Hymnal* #456, quoted in *Peacemaking Day by Day,* v. 2, Washington, DC: Pax Chrisit USA, 1989.

Pearson, Bishop Carlton. *The Gospel of Inclusion: Reaching Beyond Religious Fundamentalism to the True Love of God and Self.* New York: Atria Books, 2006.

Pelikan, Jaroslav. *Whose Bible Is It?: A Short History of the Scriptures.* New York: Viking, 2005.

Petuchowski, Jakob J. *Ever Since Sinai: A Modern View of Torah.* New York: Scribners Publications, Inc., 1961.

———. *Heirs of the Pharisees.* New York, London: Basic Books, Inc., 1970.

Plotz, David. *The Good Book: The Bizarre, Hilarious, Disturbing, Marvelous, and Inspiring Things I Learned When I Read Every Single Word of the Bible.* New York: Harper, 2008.

Potok, Chaim. *The Gift of Asher Lev.* New York: Fawcett Crest, 1990.

Pritchard, James B., ed. *Ancient Near Eastern Texts: Relating to the Old Testament.* Princeton, N.J.: Princeton University Press, 1955.

Reis, Pamela Tamarkin. *Reading the Lines: A Fresh Look at the Hebrew Bible.* Peabody, Mass.: Hendrickson Publishers, Inc., 2002.

Rubenstein, Dr. Richard L. *After Auschwitz.* Indianapolis, Ind. and New York: The Bobbs-Merrill Co., 1966.

Ruttenberg, Rabbi Danya. *Surprised by God: How I Learned to Stop Worrying and Love Religion.* Boston: Beacon Press, 2008.

Sameth, Mark. "Who Is He? He Is She: The Secret Four-Letter Name of God." *The Reform Jewish Quarterly,* Summer 2008.

Scherman, Rabbi Nosson. *The Chumash: The Torah, The Haftoros and Five Megillos with a Commentary, Anthologized from the Rabbinic Writings, The Stone Edition.* Brooklyn, New York: The ArtScroll Series published by Mesorah Publications, Ltd., 1993.

Schiendewind, William M. *How the Bible Became a Book: The Textualization of Ancient Israel.* New York: Cambridge University Press, 2004.

Schroeder, Gerald L. *The Hidden Face of God: Science Reveals the Ultimate Truth.* New York: Simon & Schuster, 2001.

———. *The Science of God: The Convergence of Science and Biblical Wisdom.* New York: Broadway Books, 1997.

Schwartz, Howard. *Tree of Souls: The Mythology of Judaism.* New York: Oxford University Press, 2004.

Shanks, Hershel, ed. *Ancient Israel: A Short History from Abraham to the Roman Destruction of the Temple.* Englewood Cliffs, N.J.: Prentice Hall, 1988.

Silverman, Morris, ed. *Sabbath and Festival Prayerbook.* New York: The Rabbinical Assembly, 1946.

Sitchin, Zecharia. *The 12th Planet: Book I of the Earth Chronicles.* Rochester, Vt.: Bear & Co., 1991.

Smith, Huston. *The Soul of Christianity: Restoring the Great Tradition.* New York: HarperSanFrancisco, 2005.

Smith, Mark S. *The Origins of Biblical Monotheism: Israel's Polytheistic Background and the Ugaritic Texts.* New York: The Oxford Press, 2001.

———. *The Early History of God: Yahweh and the Other Deities in Ancient Israel.* 2nd ed. Grand Rapids, Mich.: William B. Eerdmans Publishing Company, 2002.

Soncino Classics Collection: Talmud, Midrash Rabbah, and Zohar. CD-ROM. Davka Corporation and Soncino Press.

Spangler, Ann. *Praying the Names of God: A Daily Guide.* Grand Rapids, Mich.: Zondervan, 2004.

Spong, John Shelby. *Jesus for the Non-Religious.* New York: HarperOne, 2007.

———. *A New Christianity for a New World: Why Traditional Faith Is Dying and How a New Faith Is Being Born.* New York: HarperSanFrancisco, 2001.

———. *Rescuing the Bible from Fundamentalism: A Bishop Rethinks the Meaning of Scripture.* New York: HarperOne, 1992.

———. *Why Christianity Must Change or Die: A Bishop Speaks to Believers in Exile.* New York: HarperOne, 1999.

Stone, Merlin. *When God Was a Woman.* New York: Barnes & Noble Books, 1976.

Strand, Clark. *How to Believe in God: Whether You Believe in Religion or Not.* New York: Doubleday, 2008.

Tanakh, The Holy Scriptures: A New Translation According to the Traditional Hebrew Text. Philadelphia, Pa.: Jewish Publication Society, 1985

Trachtenberg, Joshua. *Jewish Magic and Superstition: A Study in Folk Religion.* New York: A Temple Book, Atheneum, 1970.

Van Der Torn, Karel. *Scribal Culture and the Making of the Hebrew Bible.* Cambridge, Mass: Harvard University Press, 2007.

Van Seters, John. *The Life of Moses: The Yahwist as Historian in Exodus–Numbers.* Louisville, Ky.: Westminster/John Knox Press, 1994.

———. *Prologue to History: The Yahwist as Historian in Genesis.* Louisville, Ky.: Westminster/John Knox Press, 1992.

Walsch, Neale Donald. *What God Wants: A Compelling Answer to Humanity's Biggest Question.* New York: Atria Books, 2005.

Walton, John H. *Ancient Near Eastern Thought and the Old Testament: Introducing the Conceptual World of the Hebrew Bible.* Grand Rapids, Mich.: Baker Academics, 2006.

Warren, Rick. *The Purpose-Driven Life: What on Earth Am I Here For?* Grand Rapids, Mich.: Zondervan, 2002.

Waugh, Alexander. *God.* New York: Thomas Dunne Books, St. Martin's Press, 2002.

Wellhausen, Julius. *Prolegomena to the History of Israel.* Atlanta, Ga.: Scholar's Press, 1994.

Whitman, Walt. "We Two, How Long We Were Fool'd" in *Leaves of Grass.*

Wiesel, Elie. Quoted by Alice L. Eckardt in "Rebel Against God." *Face to Face,* 6 (Spring 1979).

Wilkinson, Bruce. *The Prayer of Jabez: Breaking Through to the Blessed Life.* Sisters, Ore.: Multnomah Publishers, 2000.

Wilkinson, Darlene. *The Prayer of Jabez for Women: Breaking Through to the Blessed Life.* Sisters, Ore.: Multnomah Publishers, 2002.

Wolpe, David J. *Why Faith Matters.* New York: HarperOne, 2008.

Wordsworth, William. "Ode to Intimations of Immortality."

Wright, Robert. *The Evolution of God.* New York: Little, Brown and Company, 2009.

Zeitlin, Aaron, *zt"l.* "If You Look at the Stars and Yawn." Translated by Emanuel Goldsmith.

Zornberg, Avivah Gotlieb. *The Murmuring Deep: Reflections of Biblical Unconscious.* New York: Schocken Books, 2009.

INDEX

BOOKS OF RELATED INTEREST

Sanctuary of the Divine Presence
Hebraic Teachings on Initiation and Illumination
by J. Zohara Meyerhoff Hieronimus, D.H.L.

Kabbalistic Teachings of the Female Prophets
The Seven Holy Women of Ancient Israel
by J. Zohara Meyerhoff Hieronimus, D.H.L.

Qabbalistic Magic
Talismans, Psalms, Amulets, and the Practice of High Ritual
by Salomo Baal-Shem

The Temple of Solomon
From Ancient Israel to Secret Societies
by James Wasserman

Kabbalah and the Power of Dreaming
Awakening the Visionary Life
by Catherine Shainberg

Kabbalistic Tarot
Hebraic Wisdom in the Major and Minor Arcana
by Dovid Krafchow

Kabbalistic Healing
A Path to an Awakened Soul
by Jason Shulman

The Universal Kabbalah
by Leonora Leet, Ph.D.

INNER TRADITIONS • BEAR & COMPANY
P.O. Box 388
Rochester, VT 05767
1-800-246-8648
www.InnerTraditions.com

Or contact your local bookseller